Evolution of Education in India
A historical perspective

Lachhman Dass Bhimbat

Editor: Randeep Wadehra

ISBN-13: 978-1475100563
ISBN-10: 1475100566

Contents

Avant-propos

It was an overwhelming wish of my wife, Mrs. Adarsh, Advocate, that the manuscript of the four books handed over to her by her late father, Principal Lachhman Dass Bhimbat, be published so that the people of the country may know about their great cultural heritage. My late father-in-law had handed over the manuscript of aforesaid books to her in 1965, weeks before his demise, as he was confident that she can get it published and properly distributed.

The manuscript was in longhand. There were several cuttings and interlineations. It was a tough job to edit the same. She and our three children – Mrs. Anita Chaudhary, District & Sessions Judge, Haryana; Shri Arun Walia, Senior Additional Advocate General, Haryana; and Shri Arvind Walia, Real Estate Developer of great repute at Delhi – made great efforts to accomplish the job. Dr. Rajiv Dosanjh, an eminent Orthopaedist and a family friend, came to our rescue. He suggested the name of Shri Randeep Wadehra for this purpose. We approached Shri Wadehra and he readily agreed to do the job. He did it and found the material of great value and source of great knowledge for research scholars and the general public.

The book contains research material. It is a source for further research. Mrs. Adarsh, in her own humble way, has dedicated this book to the nation, especially to those who are interested in the search for knowledge regarding the great cultural past of our beloved country.

Harbhagwan Singh
Senior Advocate
18 May, 2011

Foreword

My father, the late Shri Lachhman Dass Bhimbat, was a dedicated educationist, a visionary, a thinker and a patriot of the highest order. His whole life was a saga of sacrifice, service to his country and the society at large.

Our family belongs to Hoshiarpur in Punjab. My paternal grandfather, Shri Faqir Chand Bhimbat, was a highly respectable citizen of Hoshiarpur. He was eager to give the best possible education to his son. He sent him to Lahore for graduation. In the pre-Partition India Lahore was the capital of the united Punjab as well as the educational and cultural capital of North India. He not only graduated with first division but also did it with honours.

After completing his education he joined the foreign service in the erstwhile princely State of Patiala as a Class-I officer. He also acted as a Deputy Foreign Minister for some time. However, he was not comfortable with the trappings of privileged lifestyle – imbued as he was with patriotic fervor. Consequently, he resigned his lucrative and secure government job and began participating in patriotic and political activities with gusto at Hoshiarpur. His speeches and other political activities were not to the liking of the district administration. Consequently he fell foul with the British rulers. As luck would have it, around that time, he got an offer from Nairobi (Kenya) to join the education service of Kenya. However, when he was abroad, he closely followed the happenings in his motherland through the radio, newspapers and other publications. My mother died in 1938 when I was just five years old; my younger brother Devinder was three years younger to me. After the death of our mother we went to Kenya and joined our father at Nairobi.

Shri Lachhman Dass served as a teacher in the only government school at Nairobi. He also served with distinction as the Principal of the prestigious Sanatan Dharam High School and Arya Samaj High School. All those who came into contact with him as students or colleagues became his ardent admirers and continued to respect him as an ideal man and an ideal teacher. I have met several of his former students who have nothing but reverence for him even today and nurture a sense of devotion for their late teacher. Many treat him as their mentor in their respective careers even after his death. He put his vast knowledge on paper in long hand. I have eleven volumes of this manuscript – averaging 50,000 words per volume; this, indeed, is an indication of how strongly he felt about the past, present and future of his beloved motherland. His arena of studies was extensive and eclectic, which, inter alia, included Indian history, culture, sculpture and the educational system in ancient India. In his writings there are exhaustive suggestions for establishing good administration and ideal educational system in India. He was convinced that India's educational system can be redeemed only if it gets its Indian soul back. It was painful for him to watch our youth mouthing western catchwords while shunning ideal work ethics. In this volume he has given several instances of how we can hold our own in the comity of nations by being truly educated in the best scholarly traditions of India.

For one reason or the other the matter regarding the publication of various manuscripts of his books could not be started till the beginning of 2009. Dr. Rajiv Dosanjh, a family friend, read a part of the manuscript and suggested the name of a friend who could edit my father's books. We discussed the matter in the family i.e. with our daughter Anita Chaudhary, now District and Sessions Judge in Haryana, our son Arun Walia, Senior Additional Advocate General, Haryana, and our younger son Arvind Walia, a real estate developer of repute. The entire family wholeheartedly approved the suggestion and consequently the matter of editing the same was entrusted to Shri Randeep Wadehra, a poet, author as well as a columnist with The Tribune. Our whole family is thankful to Shri Randeep Wadehra for editing the manuscript and omitting such passages as had become redundant because of the passage of time. The final draft was read and re-read by me and my husband Mr. Harbhagwan Singh, Senior Advocate and approved & liked it.

Shri Randeep Wadehra has put in stupendous work in the preparation and editing of the final manuscript of the first volume of the book written by my great father. I am confident that this book will be a dependable reference book for scholars and laypersons alike, not to mention our policy makers. If the contents of this book help our policy makers to take a renewed look at the way education is provided and managed in the country my father (in his heavenly abode) will feel vindicated. I am confident that it will be a great solace for the saintly soul of the late teacher and scholar.

Adarsh

Preface

Education in India is a hoary tradition. The *gurukulas* of 200 BC, the ancient Buddhist *viharas*, the mediaeval *maktabs* and *madarsas*, and the modern education system – a direct result of the British rule… going by the bounteousness of inputs one would have thought that the present mess in our education system should have been impossible to concoct. Theoretically at least the Indian society should have been fully literate and an enlightened entity. Alas, the truth is quite to the contrary. What went wrong, is there a remedy? The author, Shri Lachhman Dass Bhimbat, recommends inculcating enduring Indian values among the students – so that they may prove to be not only healthy and learned individuals but also assets to the society at large. Similarly, the teachers too need to be turned into ideal nation-builders rather than mere salaried professionals.

When we became independent the literacy rate hovered between 18% and 20%, i.e., more than 80% of the populace floundering in the darkness of ignorance; quite a soul sapping specter that! Quantitatively speaking, indeed giant strides have been taken towards making India literate. Yet, one can't help wondering whether the picture could not have been much brighter, qualitatively speaking.

Before the independence several individuals and institutions had tried to set up a functional primary education structure in the country. For example, Shri Gopal Krishna Gokhale introduced a bill in the Imperial Legislative Council in 1910 to make education free and compulsory for boys in the age group of 6–10 years. In 1944 Sir John Sargent had envisaged a plan to provide education to all between the age group of 10 to 40 years. The pre-primary education for children between three and six years was to be free and compulsory. The Sargent Report was emphatic that adult education was an essential prerequisite to the success of primary education. For adults, both general as well as vocational education was recommended. Great emphasis was also laid upon proper training for teachers. After the independence the importance of universal education was reiterated by the Dr. Radhakrishnan Commission on

University Education, the Mudaliar and Kothari Commissions, and the enunciation of the National Policy of Education at different points of time viz., 1968, 1979 and 1986 [revised in 1992]. However, our education system remains a flawed arrangement that stunts the students' intellectual growth, discourages the flowering of inherent genius and largely encourages barren elitism – a caricature of westernized colonial clones.

The present HRD Minister Shri Kapil Sibal's pronouncements on the need to reform our education system, as well as the Yashpal Committee Report, have revived the age-old debate. Why concentrate on higher education alone? Our primary as well as high school levels of education need urgent attention too. In fact, the entire superstructure of the country's education needs to be reworked. It is a gargantuan task indeed.

The media has been debating the various aspects of educational reforms, viz., *His next class act* By Shekhar Gupta, (The Indian Express dated 30 May, 2009); *Delivery is in the detail* By Pratap Bhanu Mehta (IE dated Jun 08, 2009); and *Set the campus free* by Ila Patnaik IE Jun 02, 2009. Similarly, from 02 July onwards The Tribune too had initiated a lively debate on India's education policy. However, most of these articles address the material aspect of education – with emphasis on market driven education system becoming more prominent lately – and ignore the spiritual aspect entirely. Shri Lachhman Dass Bhimbat argues passionately but cogently for resurrecting the soul of Indian education system. Although this manuscript was written between mid 1950s to early 1960s, his suggestions for improving the overall education system in the country remain relevant even today.

Shri Lachhman Dass Bhimbat, has provided forceful arguments to prove that the Sargent Report was flawed and not without hidden agenda. In fact Shri Bhimbat has provided an informed critique of not only the Sargent Report but also of Gandhiji's Wardha Scheme as well as the learned essays/proposals by other luminaries like Shri Gopal Krishna Gokhale, Lala Lajpat Rai, Lala Hardayal, P.M. Mehta and Annie

Besant et al even as he briefly dwells upon the Japanese and Soviet systems of education.

The author has given forthright reasons for the fall of Indian education system during the Muslim rule in the medieval period and its ultimate destruction during the British Raj. To place his arguments in proper perspective I have included two articles by contemporary writers in the book's Appendix. These are: *Muslims and Education* By Dr. Asghar Ali Engineer; and *Madrasa Education in India – Is it to sustain medieval attitude among Muslims?* By Shri R. Upadhyay.

Interestingly, what Indians understand as 'Muslim' or 'Islamic' attitude towards culture and books is looked upon as 'Arabic' in many Muslim countries like Turkey and Iran. To buttress my argument I cite the well researched travelogue-cum-autobiography, *Stranger to History*, by Aatish Taseer, which captures the subtle cultural/civilizational differences among Muslim countries thus exploding the myth of a homogenous global Islamic entity. To illustrate how deeply Iranians feel about their pre-Islamic civilizational heritage I quote the following lines from Taseer's tome (**Pp. 130-31**): *Then, with no warning, Muhammad asked me if I knew who Cyrus, the classical Persian king, was. It was a shift in conversation that reflected the extent to which the new regime was a reminder of old, historical wounds.*

'The Achaemenian king? Yes.' Cyrus the Great in the sixth century BC founded what became a vast global empire, the first of its kind, and whose further expansion led to the legendary wars with Greece.

'Cyrus two thousand five hundred years ago had laws that today are displayed in the United Nations!' Muhammad exploded. 'He set out human rights and said that no human being has the right to enslave other beings. This was two thousand five hundred years ago! And these mullahs try and tell us that if the Arabs hadn't come and saved us we'd be eating ants now.'

Muhammad was talking about much more than politics now. I was amazed by the freshness of this fifteen-hundred-year-old history, resurrected by the Islamic revolution in Iran. The awareness Iranian Muslims had of the time before Islam, and their conversion, didn't exist among the sub-continent's Muslims, most of whom believed they came with the Muslim invader...

'And you know what's worst?' Muhammad cried. *'They burnt our libraries and books. They tried to kill Farsi!'* *'Avicenna was a Persian writing in Arabic!'*

Evolution of Education in India: a historical perspective harks back to our civilizational glory in the field of education in an attempt to revive our traditional attitude towards education even as we assimilate the latest and the best in this field in order to resume our traditional leadership in the field of pedagogy. As the author has emphasized in this volume, there was a time when students from as far as Greece and China – as well as other parts of the world – used to take pride in studying in our educational institutions. We need to resurrect that glory. This volume emphatically advocates that this can be achieved if we marry our traditional systems with the avant-garde.

Randeep Wadehra

Introduction

India's indigenous education system had flourished during the pre-medieval times. There was a structured imparting of education to pupils from different socio-economic backgrounds. Great progress was made in the fields of philosophy, medicine, astronomy, economics, administration, pure as well as applied sciences, and arts and crafts. Scholars from distant lands came to India to have the best of education at universities like Nalanda, Takshshila and others. However, with the dawn of Muslim rule our institutions were systematically destroyed and replaced with Arabic ones. This wrought untold damage to our inherent genius and its flowering. Education suffered the most because, unlike our liberal, holistic and secular approach to academics, the Islamic education system was centered on theological dogmas which gave primacy to the Book. Therefore, contrary to scientific evidence, the earth remains flat even to this day – it would be heresy to assert otherwise in an Islamic dispensation.

But Muslim rulers and fundamentalists were not the only culprits. It is important to recall how the British Raj and its rather hasty exit from India affected the country's education system. The manner in which generations of Indian youth thought and behaved was largely, if not wholly, influenced by what can only be termed as the British Imposed Education System.

While we shall be discussing the evolution of education system in India in detail we shall also attempt at coming up with suggestions to fashion a system that would enable the country to eradicate, as soon as possible, all evils that have penetrated our present system of education and also our social system through foreign domination and infiltrations.

Chapter I

Alien rule: the consequences

The Muslim invaders and, later on, the Islamic orthodoxy during the Muslim rule, destroyed huge quantities of our precious literature, including specialized texts on various subjects like philosophy, sciences and arts, and our magnificent world famous universities; in the process, they also tried to obliterate all the factors that contributed towards our self-belief and pride as a civilization, viz., our culture, our freedom of conscience and our unity. The aliens inflicted untold hardships and cruelty upon our nation by way of forced conversions, forced marriages, loot and massacres; in many places, especially Rajasthan, countless *jauhars*[1] were performed whereby thousands of women had to jump into fire to protect their honor while their men-folk went into the battlefields knowing fully well that they would not return alive. Kidnapping and forced marriages of our womenfolk, which is the most humiliating and brutal of this sad story, were frequent and systematic. With this sort of barbaric mindset there was hardly any scope for constructive steps in the field of education.

The effects of European domination, however, were much more subtle but ruinous and far-reaching. The European domination destroyed our village system and with it our pre-British educational system – or whatever was left of it – and replaced it with their own system which demoralized, de-nationalized and de-spiritualized India. It also tried to replace our culture with European culture. The British suppressed all idea of national language, and with it our unity and solidarity as a nation, by encouraging English language and provincial vernaculars of India – as mediums of instruction as well as official communication. It distorted our bright history and pooh-poohed our splendid accomplishments and traditions. Our precious Sanskrit literature, which had providentially escaped the matchstick of the medieval invaders, was either marginalized or taken away to grace the bookshelves of libraries in the West.

In fact our very social structure was systematically subverted thanks to the denigration of our time-tested precepts and practices. Our local industry was destroyed, which spelt ruin on our economy as the burden of the whole nation of 40 crores of people now fell upon agriculture alone, thus bringing the farmer to the point of annihilation. The British regime poisoned our educational as well as social systems insidiously by introducing and institutionalizing communalism. It tried to destroy, rather successfully, the Indian ethos along with its cultural unity.

The major aim of this book is, however, not to deride the actions of our former alien rulers, but to understand the extent of damage wrought on our indigenous structure and institutions of education. Once we comprehend this only then would we be able to build a system more in tune with our ethos that would cater to our needs.

Chapter II

Perspectives on education

Lala Hardayal[2], a great Indian patriot, who had dedicated his entire life to the service of India and died in exile in America, has defined education as "a process of training and development that enables individuals or nations to make the best use of the faculties which they have been endowed with".

On the ethical aspect of education he says, "A long process of historical evaluation has resulted in the formation of well-defined, compact social groups which are marked off from one another by distinct and unmistakable features relating to manners and customs, language and religion, history and social environments. These groups of men associated together in states, tribes, *jirgahs* or clans are called nations ... An ideal system of education should satisfy the following conditions:

(1) It must awaken in boys a sense of their duty to humanity and the nation;

(2) It must form national type of character;

(3) It must accustom boys to the national modes of life and thought around them; and

(4) It must make them fit for some form of activity by which they should develop their nature and carry out their Dharma, i.e., honest livelihood by being integral part of the national machinery.

"Education must therefore be given with the history of the race to which the boy belongs... All that the race has done is its treasure, the deeds it has wrought, the thoughts it has perfected, the emotions it has felt, the arts it has developed, the revolutions it has undergone... Awakening of patriotism through teaching of national history is thus the first requisite of a sound education system. Livelihood for its own sake and at any cost seems to me the watchword of education in India at present. Bread and butter take precedence over Dharma. They who run only after bread shall lose it but those who follow Dharma will obtain both *'Artha'* and 'Kama' as promised by the sage in Mahabharata. This then is the first test which must be applied to any profession – is it socially beneficial? Does it involve any serious breach of the moral law?"

According to Swami Vivekananda "The only true teacher is he who can immediately come down to the level of the student; and transfer his soul to the student's soul and see through the student's eyes and hear through his ears and understand through his mind. Such a teacher can really teach and none else. All these negative, breaking down, destructive teachers that are in the world can never do any good."

The Soviet Russian system of education[3]

Several years ago Deana Levin had authored, *Children in Soviet Russia,* in which she had examined one Anglo-American school in Moscow. While discussing the educational system of what was then the Soviet Russia she talks about the approach to children in the system. A Russian teacher is advised not to be too strict to make the children afraid of her. If she is too strict they would not ask her questions or discuss their difficulties with her after school, and would not respect her and love her. A teacher should not have a high wall between her and children. She should let them look upon her as a person and not fear her as a teacher. Soviet Russia aimed at self-discipline which could be arguably developed in an atmosphere of comradeship and justice.

Deana Levin further says that according to the Soviet Russian System of education "a teacher whose aim is only to impart knowledge is a useless teacher and such a teacher is not respected. She must be an educator, an up-bringer and have a sound character training as well as good academic knowledge. She must study and help each child individually.

"Soviet education further aims at producing all round cultured man and woman. The word 'culture' is used in a broad sense to include all the refinements and appreciation for the arts which have come down through the ages as well as the development of the highest qualities in man and woman. With the rapid development of Soviet industry and agriculture there is an ever greater demand for highly qualified workers of every description. Further, this development aims at making machines the servants of man and thus giving him more and more leisure time. Education must therefore be for leisure as well as a qualification for work.

"The school curriculum must provide for the needs of society, must see that the pupils have a good basic knowledge for becoming highly qualified and in addition that they have a good cultural background with which they can enjoy their leisure time. The subjects taught must have a firm scientific basis in accordance with the moral principles of Marxist philosophy.

"The sciences must be mastered in order to have an understanding of natural phenomena. Without history no one can have an understanding of the events taking place in the world today, nor realize how the whole structure of present day society came into being. Geography gives knowledge of physical conditions and, linked with history, shows how physical conditions influenced political growth and caused the world to be in the condition in which it is today. The natural sciences, including botany, zoology, physiology, geology and evolution, give a complete picture of the development of life on the earth. The knowledge of human body and its functions helps to create a balanced mind and a healthy attitude towards sex. Children must master their native language and understand its literature. They must be able to express themselves well as well as to understand the rich literary heritage of the past. They should also know foreign languages and literature, for this helps them to be internationalists in spirit. Sports and gymnastics develop a strong body while music and art help understand the development of the arts and also give a means of enjoying the leisure time, which is becoming more and more possible for the farmers and workers of the Soviet Union.

"Soviet educationists believe in giving their children a sound academic training, but such a training is nothing if not supported by what may be translated as 'the upbringing of the child', i.e., a training of the character and the development of willpower, courage and courtesy, together with all the other qualities which go into the making of a balanced person. This upbringing also includes the development of patriotism towards the Socialist Fatherland, international solidarity with children throughout the world, a hatred for fascism – in short, everything that will go into the making of a good Soviet citizen.

"Every school must have its general upbringing plan which includes different activities, lectures, discussions and suggestions to teachers as to how they can carry out their aims through their ordinary lessons, never losing sight of the fact that the lesson must have a double aim - academic and educational, i.e., the material studied must be linked up with problems of life itself.

"The pioneer organization is a vital part of school life. Its aims are to raise the standard of studies, strengthen the self-discipline of the pupils and the training of their character".

In studying different systems of education, one must be acquainted with the general and common ideas about education, as well as with the different instincts of each separate race or nation – this is important to make each system of education both natural and suitable to the soil concerned.

The Japanese system of education

The book, *Japanese Education*, is a collection of lectures delivered, some decades ago, in the University of London by Baron Dairoku Kikuchi, Hon. Professor of the Imperial University of Tokyo, President of the Imperial University of Kyoto and of the Imperial University of Tokyo; sometimes Minister of Education in Japan. It contains the Imperial Rescript[4] on Education which became the basis of Japanese Education. It may be of some interest to the readers and is therefore given below:

"... Be filial to your parents, affectionate to your brothers and sisters, as husbands and wives harmonious, as friends true; bear yourselves with modesty and moderation; extend your benevolence to all; pursue learning and cultivate arts, and thereby develop intellectual faculties and perfect moral powers;

furthermore advance public good and promote common interests; always respect the Constitution and observe the laws; should emergency arise offer yourselves courageously to the State..."

Chapter III

The proposed Indian system of education

History of Indian Education through the ages

This Chapter has been subdivided under five heads:

I. The *Gurukula* system of ancient times (Vedic & Epic Periods)
II. The Medieval system of education.
III. The Pre-British system of education
IV. The Britain-Imposed System of education and why it should go
V. Some recent trends in Indian education

I. The Gurukula System of Ancient Times (The Vedic & Epic periods)

Life in the Gurukula

Let us now see how education was imparted in our country in the past. This will afford us an opportunity to study the genius of the Indian nation. During the period, usually referred to by western scholars as prehistoric or ancient times, there were swathes of forests all over India where ascetics or *Sanyasis* lived a reclusive life, far from towns. These *Rishis* (sages) lived in simple huts and spent their time practicing great austerities and studying *Vedas*, writing *Upanishads*, *Smritis* and books on Indian philosophy. They also wrote other precious books, namely, *Brahamanas* & *Aranyakas*. In this manner they made very valuable contributions to the science of metaphysics. Importantly, they also engaged themselves as teachers. Their schools called

25

Gurukulas (literally, the families of Gurus) were open to boys of all classes and ranks who accepted the simple and disciplined life of the *Ashramas*. Thus princes shared the huts, as well as the simple food, with sons of poor people. Lord Krishna, a prince during the later part of the Epic Age, and Sudama, a poor Brahmin's son, were great friends as well as fellow students in the same *Gurukula*[5]. All students went to the nearby villages and towns for alms, off which they and their teachers lived.

This practice of living on charity was useful in curbing their pride, thus placing them all on a plane of equality and humility. All of them, without exception, helped to bring dry wood from the forest as fuel for cooking and for *Havan Yajna*; they served the teachers with full devotion. The teachers also looked upon the boys as their own sons and bestowed upon them individual attention for their intellectual, moral and physical development.

The Gurukula equipment and scheme of studies

The Gurukulas were not housed in magnificent school buildings, having special furniture or any other equipment in the modern sense. The instruction was imparted in open air under rich, leafy and sun-blocking canopies of huge trees. The teacher (*guru*) sat on a leopard skin on a raised platform under a tree, while the pupils (*shishyas*) sat in front of him on their small mats (*asanas*) spread on the ground.

In these *rishi ashramas Vedas, Upanishads, Darshan Shastras* and *Smriti Granthas* etc were taught. The princes were taught the use of arms as additional subject. The course of teaching covered basic knowledge of almost all the sciences and arts. (*Vedas* are believed to be the storehouse of principles of knowledge of all modern sciences, fine arts and industrial skills, cattle breeding and agriculture, besides metaphysics, theology and moral law). Pupils joined the school at the age of ten or eleven and left the school at the age of 24 or 25 years; some of them continued their studies up to the age of 36 or even 48. During their studentship they observed *brahmcharya* (celibacy). After graduating the pupils led married lives while a few took to *sanyas*[6]. During their course of study they acquired skills in arts and crafts which helped them earn their livelihood later on as householders. The pupils were given a moral foundation with the teaching of *yamas* and *niymas*, the basic moral principles of the Indian way of life and culture. The pupils were taught *agnihotra*[7]; every morning the forests rang with the chants of *Vedic mantras* and the sweet smell of incense spread everywhere and purified the atmosphere, even causing rains. Contrast this with the modern western education, whose scientific experiments poison the atmosphere for hundreds of miles, and whose scientific research work has created deadly toxins, bacteriological and nuclear bombs not to mention guided missiles, capable of finishing off all life on this earth.

The development of pupils' physical side was not neglected in the *Gurukulas*. Every pupil was trained in yogic practices (*asanas*) and in *pranayama* or breathing exercises in the fresh forest air. The yogic *asanas* made their bodies strong and supple, facilitated control over passions. *Pranayama* helped prolong their lives, enabled them to develop self-control and thus have peace of mind. The food was *satvic*[8] and simple. It provided health, strength, enlightenment and peace of mind. It consisted of milk and butter, which was in abundance because the *ashramas* had plenty of cows; vegetables and fruits were grown in plenty in the surrounding forest areas. The *brahmcharis* received flour, rice and pulses etc from neighboring villages or from the ruling princes nearby. The food prepared from these ingredients further strengthened their vow of celibacy (*brahmcharya*). The atmosphere of simplicity, equality, hard work, continuous and vigorous academic and spiritual engagement, self denial, self control, righteousness and prayer kept their minds pure and focused, strengthened their bodies and built their character.

The students in these educational institutions were, it appears, mostly from upper castes like *Brahmins* (the priestly class) or the well-to-do *Kshatriyas* (warrior or ruling class). However, sons of *Vaishas* (the merchant and agriculturist classes) and of the *Sudras* (the labor) seldom felt interested in such education and therefore preferred to stay at home. They learnt their trade, craft or art from family elders or through the guild system. Their moral education consisted of listening to sermons or *kathas* in temples from time to time delivered by sages and the *snatakas* from the *Gurukulas*; in addition they read religious books if they became literate through private independent effort. Character development of the students of *Gurukulas* had a wholesome effect on the society at large.

The idea expressed by Lala Lajpat Rai[9] in his book, *Unhappy India*, cannot be ignored. But his "earliest times" may not be going far away enough into the *Vedic* age. He says:

a.   "From the earliest times there was a well organized and widespread system of education throughout India.

b.   That this system was two-fold – one for the aristocratic, cultured and priestly classes aiming at religious learning and culture (perhaps here he refers to the *Gurukula* system), the other for the trading and working classes aiming at economic efficiency and dexterity in the use of tools (something akin to the system of apprenticeship in Tudor-England. These schools were run perhaps, nearer home, in the villages themselves – Author).

c.   That this system, as a part of our village tradition, had lasted as a living organization till the British occupancy of this country.

"Possibly, there was a parallel system of education in the villages, having separate arrangement for girls, and for those who could not accept the hard disciplined life of the *Gurukula* system. At any rate the demand for popular education had reached a high watermark at the beginning of the *Sutra* Age[10] of the Renaissance Period. The great material prosperity of the country, the phenomenal progress in arts and crafts, the expansion of internal and external trade, proper organization of the Indian navy, the great conquests of foreign countries by Indian kings (*Chakravarti Rajas*) culminating in *Rajsuya* and *Ashwamedha Yajnas*[11], the great expansion of India's colonies and settlements especially in the southeast Asia, Afghanistan and some parts of Central Asia and in Egypt and China, Greece and Italy and finally the rich literature of the Renaissance period had, I think, created a widespread and properly organized system of education.

"A great poet of *Sutra* age says: *Those who have neither education nor penance, charity, knowledge, good conduct, art and sense of moral duty, are burden on the earth; they are only lower animals in human form.*

"But this education of the Gurukula system was meant only for boys. I wonder if there was any separate arrangement on a large scale for the education of girls, in those very ancient times. According to Shri Shanti Kumar Narain Ram Vyas in his essay on *Hindu Sanskriti in Ramayana*, in the *Hindu Sanskriti Ank*, we find arrangement for girls' education and lodging in *Rishi Ashrams*. In those *Vedic* and Epic times when peace and plenty were smiling on the country and there was no such thing as the modern amoral/immoral principles of struggle for existence or the survival of the fittest, when simple living and high thinking was the rule of life, and when devotional service of the husband and proper care of children and of old relations at home was considered to be the height of perfection and attainments for a woman, the academic knowledge was perhaps considered a sort of luxury meant for a comparatively small minority. The whole atmosphere was surcharged with morality, prayer, fasts and worship. Attendance of schools by girls was consequently considered unnecessary, perhaps. She learnt from her mother and, after marriage, from her mother-in-law, the domestic science and skills for the care of children. Since cottage industries were the norm in those days girls acquired manufacturing and other industry related skills at home itself."

The system of education in *Gurukulas*, I think, was the best system for those times as it was built on the indigenous genius and met all our national needs of those times. The shining lights of that system of education and of our ancient social life that appeal to me the most and which, I think, are engrained in our blood are the lofty institutions of Yoga and its centerpiece, the *brahmcharya* besides other aspects like *yajnas* and the philosophy of *Sanskara*. No Indian system of education can be called truly national without these two potent elements of Indian social life and character. If we blindly copy the materialist West in building up our system of education, as is seen from some of our recent trends in education, we may be able to achieve the material heights that the West has already achieved but we will, in that adventure, lose the soul of India and her spiritual heights; and the genius of the nation will be ruthlessly suppressed.

The shining lights of the Gurukula System: Yoga and Brahmcharya

Now what are these two lofty institutions: the 'Yoga' and the 'Brahmcharya'?

Yoga is defined by Maharishi Patanjali[12] in his *Yoga Darshan* as control of mind as it is always restless and, monkey like, is in the habit of running hither and thither. In *Yoga Darshan*, which is otherwise known as *Ashtang Yoga* or *Rajyoga,* eight parts of *Raja Yoga* have been described. These eight parts are: (1) *Yamas* (these are five in number, viz., *ahimsa, satya, asteya, brahmcharya,* and *aprigraha*) (2) *Niyamas* (these too are five in number, viz., *shouch, santosh, tapa, swadhyaya,* and *Ishwar pranidhanam*).

The first half of the Yogic System

The first half of the yogic system covers *Yamas, Niyamas, Asanas, Pranayama* and *Pratyahara*. These *yamas* and *niyamas* are beneficial for acquiring ethical training and purification of mind.

Asanas and their uses

According to Swami Swananda, in his book *Yogic Home Exercises,* "*Asanas* are physical exercises. They develop the body. The spine becomes elastic, the body supple and the appetite vigorous. One's heart, lungs, brains and the cerebrospinal system are kept in a healthy condition. Vital forces are preserved and enhanced. Circulation of blood is kept in proper order. Spinal cord is toned up. The practice of *asanas* prevents development of arteriosclerosis or hardening of the arteries. The practice of *asanas*, in fact, lubricates the whole body system.

Other special characteristics of *asanas* are: (1) Excellent for the exercise of stomach, which is not found in other systems, and there are several diseases of stomach which are cured by *asanas*. (2) Require no tools or apparatus ordinarily; therefore economical and convenient as the exercises can be taken even when one is away from home. (3) In this system there are exercises for men, women and children and even for old and sick people. (4) These exercises steady the posture and give you complete mastery over the body".

Pranayama and its uses

Swami Swananda further says, "*Pranayama* removes diseases of the body and renovates the cells and nerves. It supplies fresh energy, purifies and steadies the mind, strengthens intellect, increases memory, calms turbulent senses and checks their wayward tendencies; it facilitates *nadi shudhdhi* (purification of the nervous system). Lungs are developed with proper supply of oxygen enabling them to successfully resist various infections including *Bacillus tuberculosis*. Blood is purified and there is improvement in its quality and quantity. All the tissues and cells are nourished with plenty of pure blood and lymph. *Pranayama* invigorates the nerves, destroys *Rajas* (passion) and *Tamas* (inertia), makes body elastic and light, energizes the heart and the circulation of the blood, improves digestion, augments the vital force and helps the liver to perform its work efficiently. Lastly, it prolongs life by strengthening the lungs and purifying and enriching the bloodstream".

Pratyahara and its uses

Pratyahara[13] literally means vomiting out or renunciation, just as *Ahara* means swallowing up of food or catching. In plain language, *Pratyahara* means liberalizing of the senses from sensual objects and through this procedure the liberalizing of the mind from both senses and sensual objects; because senses cannot enjoy sensual objects unaccompanied by mind. It is thus a succession of repeated practices of dragging the mind away from senses and sensual as well as material objects, till it becomes strong enough to resist them and bring them under control. So, *pratyahara* gives strength, peace and rest to mind; by shaking off its restlessness it is in a fit condition to concentrate upon worthier issues and objects. This makes up the elementary ethics or Yogic course for the Basic School.

Practical application of the system

The practice of *yamas, niyamas, asanas, pranayama* and *pratyahara* should be compulsory for all school children; however, the consent of the guardians and factoring in of medical test reports are essential prerequisites. To me it appears that they form an essential part of the physical and moral culture of school children.

After obtaining proficiency in the basic moral principles as well as mental and physical efficacy, most, if not all, children will be able to gradually complete the cycle of perfect life. There will be a miniscule minority, of pure *Satvic* temper – who may be described as *Yoga Bhrashtas* – who had achieved near-perfection in their previous births and now need only a stimulus in this life to launch them onto the tough and demanding, but achievable, path to *Moksha* or perfection and thus become one with the Infinite. They may take to the *Nivriti Marg* or the way of the *Sanyasi* for quick self-advancement and for the good of humanity at large. And it is for the latter, very limited number of India's children, that the last three stages of Yoga, viz., *dharana, dhyana* and *samadhi* are meant – for the most part in *Rishi Ashrams*. However, prior knowledge of these yoga exercises, after completing the basic school course and acquiring sufficient knowledge of Sanskrit and further perfecting the practice of *yamas, niyamas, asanas, pranayama* and *pratyahara*, will enable them to be quite well-equipped to join some *Vanprashta, Sanyasa* or *Rishi Ashram* for self-realization, research work and for more efficient service of humanity. This process will, incidentally, serve to stop the multiplication of fake *sanyasis* or professional beggars and pretenders in the country. This second part of the yogic course is to be given as an optional subject in the polytechnic to those who show any inclination for it. To those who enroll for this Higher Ethics course in the polytechnic it would be of immense use as they would be still better equipped with this training to focus their minds and intellect on research work of every kind in the material sphere too. And, as specialists, they would be able to solve those problems which defy solution by average intelligence.

The latter half of the Yogic System

The other half of the Yogic System covers *Dharana, Dhyana* and *Samadhi*.

Dharana or concentration has a broad meaning. It covers, on the one hand, the proper, motionless posture that facilitates concentration of mind according to *Shrimad Bhagwat Gita* and, on the other hand, it means the fixing of mind on an external object or an internal point. This enables the mind to develop psychic powers or soul force, knowledge of telepathy and intuition. Thence it gradually merges into intellect and loses its separate existence according to *Amritnad Upanishad* and *Katho Upanishad*.

Dhyana or meditation is the next step to *Dharana* or concentration. Concentration merges into meditation with daily practice. An unbroken flow of knowledge by intellect into *atma* or inner consciousness is meditation. For, at this point, no material object is of much consequence to the man who aspires to achieve salvation. This intellect now centers on the concentrated object or *atma* and gradually merges into it and loses its separate existence. This *atma*, or inner consciousness, thus in its turn, merges into the all pervading consciousness or the Infinite. This stage is called *Samadhi*. Thus, *Yoga Sadhana* or *Yogabhyas* is a process of gradual self-surrender or self-elimination like the disappearance of crystal sugar into water or like merging into the ocean of love by a small stream and, in the process, losing its separate identity. In this process, first the sensual objects leave, then the senses or, collectively, the body become less important. Thereafter, the mind leaves followed by the intellect. The soul alone is left behind, which finally takes a plunge, in sheer bliss, into the Great Infinite. This is called *Moksha*, the Indian Culture's final goal or destination.

Samadhi, according to Swami Sivanand in his book *Yogic Home Exercises*, is "super conscious state wherein the *Yogi* gets super-intuitional or super-sensual knowledge and super-sensual bliss."

Yajnavalkya[14] is quoted by Swami Sivananda as saying, "By *pranayama* impurities of the body are destroyed; by *dharana*, or concentration, the impurities of the mind; by *pratyahara* the impurities of attachment and by *Samadhi* everything that hinders the soul is removed."

Brahmcharya

According to Swami Sivananda, "*Brahmcharya* is the vow of celibacy in thought, word and deed, by which one attains self-realization and reaches Brahma. It means control of not only the reproductive *Indri* (organ) but also the control of all senses, viz., eyes, nose, ear, tongue and the reproductive organ, in thought word and deed. The door to *nirvana* or perfection or supreme peace is complete *brahmcharya*. A *brahmchari* is one who is attempting to realize Brahma by living a life of absolute celibacy. According to a Sanskrit *shloka*: '*that which is thought is spoken by the mouth, that which the mouth speaks, the organs of action do*'. Vedas say: Let my mind think of auspicious things. By *brahmcharya* penance the learned pious people have conquered death. The *Shrutis* have declared: This *atma* is not attainable by a weak man. Gita says: That desiring which *brahmcharya* is performed.

"Practice of *brahmcharya* gives good health, inner strength, peace of mind and a long life. It invigorates the mind and nerves. *Ojas Shakti* is spiritual energy that is stored up in the brain. By sublime thoughts, meditation, *japa*, worship, *asana* and *pranayama* practice, the sexual energy can be transmuted into *Ojas Shakti*. This energy can be utilized for Divine Contemplation and spiritual pursuits".

Disciplined life: A sine qua non of Yoga

"A glutton can never become a *brahmchari*. There is an intimate connection between the tongue and the reproductive organ.

"The senses must be controlled by various methods such as fasting, restriction in diet, *pranayama, japa, kirtan*, meditation, *pratyahara* or abstraction of mind from objects, *aatm-samyam* or self-control, *asanas, bandhas, mudras*, thought control and destruction of *vasanas* (desires) etc.

"Control the tongue and the lust will be controlled. Delicious *rajasic* foods excite the organ of generation.

"One drop of semen is manufactured out of 40 drops of blood according to modern medical science". According to Ayurveda it is elaborated that 80 drops of blood are used up for the purpose. Just as sugar is all-pervading in sugarcane, butter in milk, so also semen pervades the whole body (destruction of semen causes death, protection of semen supports life). Semen imparts *Brahma-Tejas* to the face and strength to the intellect."

"Just as oil is sucked up by a wick and burns with glowing light, so also the *veerya* (semen) flows upwards by the practice of *Yoga Sadhana* and is converted into *Tejas* or *Ojas*. The *Brahmchari* shines with *Brahmic* aura on his face" I want to see this *Brahmic* aura shining on the faces of India's children once again as it did in the past.

Advantages of the Yogic System

(1) The five *Yamas* are (a) *Ahimsa*, (b) *Satya* (c) *Asteya* (d) *Brahmcharya* and (e) *Aparigraha*.

(a)   *Ahimsa* or non-violence in thought, word and deed comprises, among other things, the consideration for special needs of the nation, the country, the sanctity of individual and group life and liberty. It also helps structure true democracy based on the *Panch Sheel* (the policy enunciating the 'live and let live' principle). Basically, *Ahimsa* enables one to lead a life of non-injury, or *Sadachar*. It makes a man harmless and lovable and leads to social harmony and peace. But *Ahimsa* does not imply timidity or dereliction of duty, nor does it forbid one to take up arms against the nation's enemies. For, according to *Dharma Shastras*, killing of external and internal enemies of the country is neither crime nor sin; in fact, it is a man's moral duty. Such an act has been termed as pure *Ahimsa* because it is not based on greed or selfishness. It is based on morality, justice and peace. The term "enemies" comprises six categories: (1) one who burns your houses and other property and creates chaos, lawlessness, fear and disruption; (2) one who administers poison in any way and who wants to kill you through poisoning; (3) one who invades the country;(4) one who carries off as booty your property and the womenfolk; (5) one who deprives you of your homes and property, parts of your country or tries to cause dismemberment of your country in any manner; and (6) one who kills womenfolk and innocent children. But the killing of enemies should be done without malice and in the interest of justice. This should be done with a view to protect the weak and the innocent and for the security of one's country; and to stop such rogues from committing further acts of cruelty and villainy. It is thus an act of positive mercy.

(b)   *Satya* or truthfulness in thought, word and deed, requires one to lead the life of justice, equity and good conscience and promote liberty, equality and fraternity. Truthfulness fulfills all desires through trust and friendship. It removes all anxiety and creates an atmosphere of fearlessness and joy. It makes a man believable. This *Satya* is also governed by special needs of the society, of the state and of the time.

(c)   *Asteya*, or such non-stealing in thought, word and deed as is in consonance with the needs of the society, state and times. It

36

promotes non-exploitation of the weak, non-colonialism, non-imperialism and non-racialism. It brings within your reach all precious and essential things. It gives joy and contentment. It makes one self-reliant and industrious and also helps improve the moral tone of the whole society.

(d)   *Brahmcharya,* in thought word and deed, stands for the vow of celibacy or self control or sexual morality and purity of conduct. A *brahmchari* treats all women with respect and is ordained to look upon other people's wives as his mothers. *Brahmcharya* improves one's health and prolongs life. It creates an atmosphere of high character, moral purity and domestic peace and contentment – both at the micro as well as macro levels. It enables the seeker of truth to acquire the vision of the Lord. Literally, it stands for the search for God. The advocates of *brahmcharya* firmly believe that without conservation of semen, no control and concentration of mind are possible; therefore, no vision of the Lord is possible.

(e)   *Aparigraha*[15] or dispossession also means self-denial, charity and renunciation. It is a true form of non-violent, and very much Indian, socialism that is based on social justice and social equality. It finds mention in the *Ishavasyam Upanishad*[16]. All that is seen in this wide universe is owned and occupied by God. Therefore, take your share out of that immense wealth with a sense of self-denial and contentment. Do not be greedy. Do not accept anything from others in the form of bribe, or through fraud, begging or injustice or without doing any useful work or service in return. Who but He can call it His own wealth? This *aparigraha* makes a man independent and gives him true happiness of the mind. It also helps establish the superiority of spiritual life over material life. This *aparigraha* also is governed by the special needs of the nation, the country and the times.

(2) The five *Niyamas* are: (a) *Shouch* (b) *Santosh* (c) *Tapa* (d) *Swadhyaya* and (e) *Ishwar Pranidhanam.*

(a) *Shouch* stands for purity of mind and body, i.e., internal and external purity of all kinds. It demands six practices from man: *Dhauti, Vasti, Neti, Fratak, Nauli* and *Kapalbharti*. It enables concentration of mind, control over senses and mind and develops vision of the 'Infinite'.

(b) *Santosh* or contentment that makes one look at others' wealth as clod of earth and enables one to have full faith in God's distribution of His wealth. It gives immense peace and inward happiness and the fullest of satisfaction in the justice of God.

(c) *Tapa* or penance. It covers self-control, self-denial, self-reliance, courage, fortitude, fearlessness, perseverance or endurance in danger and calm in the midst of calamities. It maintains heat in the body, creates activity and generates aura in man. *Tapa* makes forgiveness a habit while turning man into a living force.

(d) *Swadhyaya*[17] stands for search for the truth or the Infinite. It makes a man thoughtful. It helps prevent the mind from wandering among material objects and turns it inwards which is the real mission of human life. It enables man to take help from the power of God, of his own choice, for the attainment of *Moksha*.

(e) *Ishwar pranidhanam* denotes self-surrender at the feet of the Lord, to give one's self up into His hands. It facilitates submergence of one's inner consciousness into the all-pervading consciousness. It means full realization of God within the body; to think one's self or soul as not separate from, but a part of, God. It makes possible the attainment of full *Samadhi* which enables the soul to expand into the Infinity and, thus, completes the mission of human life.

These five *Yamas* and five *Niyamas* will lead to the regeneration of the individual and the world at large, ushering in purity and peace.

(3) *Asanas* improve circulation of blood. All vital organs of the body are kept in a healthy condition and the whole system is toned up.

(4) *Pranayama* strengthens lungs and purifies blood and, therefore, prolongs life. It enables the soul to have full control over senses, body and mind.

(5) *Pratyahara* sets senses free from sensual objects and the mind from senses.

(6-7)   *Dharana* and *Dhyana* establish full concentration of mind by depriving it of its habitual restlessness. *Dharana* and *Dhyana* submerge it into the soul through meditation. It, thus, loses its separate identity.

(8) *Samadhi* is the final super-conscious state when the soul submerges into the Infinite. It loses its separate existence like a raindrop from a cloud falling into the ocean – its final place of rest from where it had started its journey as a result of the evaporation process.

Salient features of the ancient Gurukula system of education

The ancient system of education, as it existed in the *Vedic* and Epic Times, had several positive features:

a) It was a purely residential system. Pupils lived with their guru or gurus for at least twelve years and sometimes for twenty four to thirty six years or even longer. The guru looked upon them as his own children, treating them as if they belonged to his family. He, therefore, took personal interest in their education, health and all-round development. "The personal relationship", as Lala Lajpat Rai says in his book, *The Problem of National Education in India*, "supplied the human element, which is now missing. This was a guarantee of greater attention being paid to the formation of habits which compose character." But, in the present education structure the teacher has been reduced to being a merchant selling the contents of certain prescribed textbooks and nothing more. His profit consists of the monthly salary he gets for his work. As the goods are delivered sometimes to very young people and there is no other adult witness for the daily transaction, the School Inspector steps in occasionally to regulate the sale. His job is to ensure that the marketing of goods goes on smoothly. In order to satisfy the students' parents, several examinations are held and examination marks-cards/reports are issued to show that the market is functioning and the work is going on smoothly. But all this propaganda of proper teaching was not required in those ancient times;

b) Physical exercise in the form of Yogic *asanas*, besides other physical activities, was an integral part of education. It had a very salutary effect on every organ of the body and its balanced development. It provided excellent health and strength to pupils.

c) Pure and well balanced *satvic* food, fresh and salubrious air of the forest, simple and disciplined life of penance and self-denial, healthy thoughts and positive worldview – all left their mark on the pupil's future life. With the passage of time this old, strict discipline apparently came to an end during the Middle Ages. Only the spiritual ideology survived which is quite alive and vibrant in the Indian social system even today.

Lala Lajpat Rai's criticism of the ancient system

Lajpat Rai, who has done a very valuable pioneering service to the cause of Indian national education, critiques the ancient system thus: "... (The ancient system of education) had a tendency of enslaving the pupil's mind. The aim of education should be to qualify the educated man to think and act for himself with a due sense of responsibility towards society. It only made mere copies of gurus. The discipline enforced was too strict, too mechanical and too empirical. The religion taught was too formal, rigid and narrow." He goes on to say that there was too much memorizing of rules of grammar and text thus wasting time. Further, he says, there was too much of segregation of the pupil from the society which was harmful in many respects, and this did not suit the ideal of popular education, i.e. education for all boys and girls of school going age without exception. Thus, no popular education, says Lajpat Rai, was possible in ancient times although there were large *Ashramas* and *Parishads* (cooperatives of several Gurus). He further observes that the institution of begging alms for themselves (pupils) and Gurus is repugnant to modern taste; self-help or partial state aid is a better alternative. The old system of segregation from society, he says, was more than neutralized by the institution of begging as pupils came into contact with females when they visited households for alms (*Bhikhsha*). The system governed by codes was not universally followed. It provided knowledge only to some of the Brahmin boys and some princes or highly placed *Khshatriyas*. He goes on: "It is detrimental to the sort of character we want to develop, nay which we must develop in our boys and girls if we want to keep pace with the rest of the world in their march onward. Our boys and girls must not be brought up in hot-houses... They (our boys and girls) should be brought up in the midst of the society of which they are to be members. They should form habits and learn manners which will enable them to rise to every emergency. They should learn to rise above temptations and not shun them.

"Boys and girls must learn their social obligations when in their teens. To segregate them at such a time is to deprive them of the greatest and the best opportunity of their lives. The idea of having schools and colleges and universities in localities far away from the bustle of city life and from the temptations incidental to it is an old idea which is being abandoned by the best educational thinkers of the world. The new idea is to let the boys and girls be surrounded by the conditions of life in which they have to move and which they have to meet in later life. To let boys and girls grow in isolation, ignorant of the conditions of actual life, innocent of its social amenities, with no experience of the sudden demands and emergencies of group life is to deprive them of the most valuable element in their education. The aim of education is to equip men and women for the battle of life. We do not want to convert them into anchorites and ascetics. The boys and girls of today are the citizens of tomorrow. From among them must come our statesmen, administrators, generals, inventors, captains of industry and manufacturers, as much as our philosophers and thinkers and teachers. Even sound thinking, to be useful for practical purposes of life, must be based on a full knowledge of the different phases of social life. All life is social. We are beginning to realize that the best social thinkers of the world have been those who were brought up in the full blaze of the social conditions of the time and who had personal experience of how men in general lived and how they acted and reacted on each other... Boys brought up in isolation and girls brought up in *purdah*[18] make very poor men and women. Often they have been seen succumbing to the first temptations they come across. They wreck their lives from want of experience and want of nerve... Not that men educated in ordinary schools and colleges are always better but that at least the former have not shown any superiority in handling situations which arise from being thrown into social conditions to which they were strangers before. My experience justifies me in saying that the latter go to greater extremes in laxity of character and looseness of behavior than the former. They lack the power of adjustment.

"... Boys and girls should be treated more as comrades rather than dependants and inferiors and subordinates. We should extend to them our fullest confidence and encourage absolute frankness in them. Instead of keeping the sexes separate we should bring them together. In my judgment greater harm is done by keeping them apart than by bringing them together. I know I am treading on debatable ground. Prejudice and sentiment accumulated over centuries of restricted life is all against it. The thing will come by degrees. But come it must and come it will.

"It will be so much waste of energy not to profit by the experience of other peoples. Our ideas of morality and decency must undergo change. Our boys and girls must grow up in an atmosphere of frankness, freedom and mutual confidence. We must do away with suspicion and distrust. It breeds hypocrisy, sycophancy and disease. The future teachers and gurus of India must learn to set aside the tone of command and authority to which they have been accustomed. The boys and girls are not clay in their hands to be molded into patterns of their choice. That was a stupid idea if ever it existed. They are living beings, products of nature, heredity and environments. ... They cannot be regulated by mere authority, without inflicting awful injury on their manhood and womanhood. We command them to do things, of the righteousness and value of which they have not been convinced. The result is a habit of slavish submission to authority. I recognize that we cannot perhaps eliminate the element of command altogether from the education and bringing up of boys and girls. They must sometimes be protected from themselves. But the command should be the last step taken with reluctance and out of a sense of unavoidability which comes by having otherwise failed to arouse an intelligent understanding in the child.

"... In short, the system that stresses the authority of the teacher or the parent, which is based on a suspicion of human nature and human tendencies, which is distrustful of childhood and youth, which is openly out for control and discipline and subordination, which favors empirical methods of pedagogy, and which has no respect for the instincts of the boy and the girl, is not an ideal system for the production of self-reliant, aggressive (in order to be progressive) men and women that new India wants. I come to the conclusion, therefore, that any widespread revival of the ancient or medieval systems of education is unthinkable. It will take us centuries back and I am certain that the country will not adopt it.

"... I know there are groups of people in India who are in love with that system. They are sometimes carried away by a partial praise of certain features of this system by eminent foreigners and educationalists. A system may be fascinating without being sound. It may be highly interesting as an experiment. It may be good for governmental purposes, yet harmful from the citizens' point of view. It may be good for producing certain types but harmful if adopted for the nation as a whole... Some of them praise out of sheer disgust with their own systems of life. They do not want to make proper comparisons but rush from one extreme to another; others only mean to pay a generous compliment. Some perhaps mean mischief.

"Truth is truth. We should take what is good in the modern scientific development, e.g. in modern sciences of medicine, surgery, pathology, hygiene, engineering (civil, mechanical, electrical, agricultural and mining), botany, geology, zoology etc. because they are so much advanced when compared to what we have in our literature on these subjects, and also in the modern sciences of navigation, commerce, banking, insurance, politics and civics and sociology. It will be sheer folly to replace the modern treatises on arithmetic, geometry, algebra, trigonometry and kindred subjects by Lilawati or other books on these subjects found in Sanskrit language. Our *Arthshashtra* is old enough. We should insist on the teaching of the modern and the up to date arithmetic which controls and orders the economic life of the world. With a view to reach at one point we should similarly found the new social philosophy in the higher studies by making a comparative study of the old Manu, Narada and Apasthamba and the Statute made laws of modern India and of other countries. A study of modern laws, of civics of the modern world, of the forms of government prevailing in other countries, of the policies and economics is a *sine qua non* of future progress on healthy lines. What about the modern science of arms and the art of war? Are we going to re-introduce the bow and arrow or the matchlock gun or fighting with swords and spears? We should shake off all soft sentimentality. We can no longer lead an isolated and self-contained life.

"The whole world is drifting to one world unity and one world culture. The Japanese have been thoroughly Europeanized. The process is almost universal. Uniformity may be hideous and there may be beauty in variety. But whether we wish it or not, variety is going to disappear, at least superficially or it will be reduced very appreciably in the course of the next two centuries. It may seem strange, it may look humiliating, but the unity of Asia is going to be brought about by Europe and European thought. Fear of Europe will unite Asia and then the fear of Asia in its turn will bring about the unity of Europe and Asia. With Europe and Asia united, the world becomes one. America is a child of Europe, and native Africa is more or less a child of Asia. Both of them, in their own ways, are going to help the process of assimilation, integration and unity. Out of the World War I will emerge world unity."

Lajpat Rai was a well traveled patriot and an eminent educationalist as he was connected with the DAV College of Lahore (now in Pakistan). He also studied at close quarters the American system of education during his exile. His experience of other nations, his knowledge of their ways of life and of the development of their educational theory and practice are our precious possessions and I quite value his guidance in several directions in our educational planning. But with all that, I think, the whole of our ancient educational system is not to be condemned outright as he has done, perhaps impressed with the material glamour of Europe and America. The wisdom, perhaps, lies between the two extremes: the isolation and hard discipline of the ancient system and the total freedom that boys and girls enjoy under the western system. If the former, in extreme form, can stunt intellectual growth then the latter ignores the fact that during adolescence one's judgment is still immature and the sense of responsibility and of discrimination between good and evil has not sufficiently developed. We cannot copy the West blindly in everything they say or do. We have to give proper consideration to our national ideology which, from times immemorial, is still shining in our social system and which is essentially different from the material ideology of the West.

Further, we have to consider the natural instinct of India, its present and future needs, the hot climate and the comparatively early dawn of puberty in this country vis-à-vis the cold West. It is all right to have coeducation in the basic classes, so that boys and girls may learn to move about together like brothers and sisters in the atmosphere of Gurukula morality, learn self-control and decency of life and of manners. This will enable them to shake off all unwholesome shyness and prejudices. Similarly, let there be coeducation at the college level in separate sections if possible. Since the pupils will be sufficiently mature and well-disciplined they will have acquired enough maturity to discriminate between good and evil, along with a heightened sense of responsibility. The whole arrangement from beginning to end will also be very economical to the nation.

But at the Polytechnic High School stage (14 to 18 years), which is the adolescent period, a partial separation may perhaps be found a little more convenient and wise. The boys and girls in this case may have the same common school, the same mixed staff and school equipment but let them sit in separate sections or class rooms. We should modernize our educational system to the fullest extent to meet all the present and future needs of the country. But, the *Yogic Asanas* and *Pranayama* exercises, the *Gurukula* atmosphere as well as the practice of *Yamas* and *Niyamas*, which are representative of Indian spiritual life and culture as well as of the genius of our nation, should not be rejected. They should rather be a part of the foundation of our new system of education.

Let our schools, therefore, have the body, the beauties and variety of the present western university life and education. But the soul, in the form of the ideals of our ancient *Gurukula* system, must be preserved. Let the East and the West, the past and the present meet in an Indian school having all the plus points of the modern western and the ancient eastern education systems with the drawbacks of none, as we have to modernize India without losing our ancient soul.

II. The Medieval System of Education

New developments in Indian social life and education

The *Gurukula* system of education went on undisturbed during the *Vedic* Age[19] as well as the Epic Age. However, during the latter part of the Epic Age[20] – around the *Mahabharata* era – there was a perceptible deterioration in the dissemination of education. Instead of pupils going to *Rishi Ashrams* for education, the *Rishis* started coming down to the pupils' residences to teach them; this denotes the changing equation between the teacher and the taught – obviously the status of the teacher had declined. In the beginning of the *Sutra* Age, or during India's Renaissance Period[21], after a span of about two thousand years of national decay, it appears, this deterioration in the system of education was further aggravated. The education centers moved from forest areas towards towns and cities. Perhaps, this was because education had become more popular among all classes of society as well as among both the sexes. New ideas were generated that released new forces, thus bringing about the Indian Renaissance, which gave birth to a variety of literature. The increasing needs of the country for education, growth in industry, the expansion of foreign markets and the growing demand for Indian artifacts and other goods in foreign lands, the widely developed Indian shipping – which resulted in Indian merchants coming in contact with foreign nations – all generated demand for highly skilled and educated labor force as well as entrepreneurs. The urge for equal opportunities for education for girls within the country was strengthened by the shaking up of the *Varan Ashram* system after the *Mahabharata* War. The teachings of Lord Buddha[22] and Mahavir Swami[23], stressing upon *Karma* and *Gyana*, too were significant contributing factors. All cities and towns were humming with educational activity and female education also was in the forefront. It is said that debates on theology and philosophy were sometimes presided over by women. It is a matter of common knowledge that in a theological/philosophical debate between Shankaracharya and Bharati[24], the learned wife of Mandana Mishra, she had disarmed him. Several women had achieved a high degree of proficiency in poetry, mathematics, music and dance. The heads of states also, with a view to make their states politically strong, began to take more interest in education. It, however, seemed to have lost some of its old simplicity and hard discipline. The cultural foundations and the spiritual element, however, had remained intact but more importance came to be attached to technology, fine arts and crafts. Indians have been expert ship-builders from *Vedic* times and there was a lot of internal and external trade which made the country very prosperous. Along with trade, Indian culture spread to several countries of Asia, Europe and Northern Africa long before the dawn of *Sutra* Age – even during the Epic Age. During the reign of Gupta Dynasty education in the country had reached the highest pitch of excellence. Students from foreign countries came to India for education. Mahamahopadhyaya Gauri Shankar Hari Chand Ojha, to whom I am very much indebted for a lot of information for the Rajput Period (600 AD to 1200 AD) mentions in his useful book *Madhya Kaleen Bhartiya Sanskriti*, "Buddhist teachers and Hindu ascetics taught with full zeal and devotion in *Mathas* also called *Sangharamas*[25]. There were several *Sangharamas* in every big city."

Huentsang[26], a Chinese traveler, writes that in one city, Kannauj, in what is now the Indian Union's state of Uttar Pradesh, several thousand students were receiving education. In Mathura, another city in Uttar Pradesh, there were about two thousand students. From the accounts given by Chinese travelers it appears that Bharat had about five thousand *Mathas* or *Vidyalayas* with 2,12,130 students on their rolls. Besides these great institutions there were numerous other small schools run by learned Brahmins and Jain teachers in their homes. To add to these, there were big Universities or *Vishwa Vidyalayas*, carried on by heads of various States and also by the public. The chief among them were Nalanda in Bihar, Takhshila (Texla) in Punjab, Vikram Shil in Bihar and Dhan Katak in the Deccan. There were also other universities smaller than these in other parts of the country, viz. at Banaras, Vidarbha, Ajanta and Ujjain. Banaras and Vidarbha universities were strongholds of the Vedic knowledge and philosophy. Ujjain University was world famous for astronomy and Ajanta University for the teaching of arts. The facade of one of the ruined buildings of Ajanta bears testimony to the excellence of the art that was taught here. Education was free. On the other hand, the students' other expenses also were met by these universities. Clothing, medicine, boarding and lodging were all free.

In Nalanda University, founded just after Buddha's death, located near the present Nalanda railway station, there were arrangements for every kind of instruction, i.e. literature, philosophy, fine arts, medicine etc. It is said that scholars came from distant lands like China, Japan, Tatar, Central Asia, Tibet, Siam, Anam, Burma and Malaya. Such was the prestige of this university in the world that education was not considered complete without becoming a graduate from this University. High walls in ruins, innumerable heaps of earth, and parts of old tanks can be seen today, which tell a sad story of its ancient glory. One statue, probably of Naga Arjuna (or, Nagarjuna), the founder of the Mahayana sect of Buddhism, has also been found there as it was the centre of that sect. In that university alone, according to Huentsang, there were about ten thousand students, one hundred lecture rooms, very big blocks of dormitories, four storeys high, and one thousand five hundred teachers. The university had a very strict monastic discipline. Students were not permitted to talk to a woman or to see one; even a desire to look upon a woman was considered a great sin and was punished. In the morning every student was desired to bathe in the great swimming pool; there were ten such great pools in the University. The course of study was for twelve years but some students stayed for thirty years and some for life as research scholars. The state had assigned the revenues of about two hundred *gramas* (towns and villages) for its financial support. Connected with the university in Bihar alone, there were eight big sections and three hundred subsections. The Senate was divided into ten bodies. There were 300 hostels for students, three big libraries named as *Ratna Sagar, Ratan Dadhi* and *Ratan Ranjak*. There was a good Meteorological Observatory located in the university's premises. There was also one water clock (*Jalghari*). One had to pass tough entrance test to secure admission to the university. But during the last days of Nalanda University, the worst form of *Bajrayana*[27] or immorality (which finally overtook Buddhism in India and led to its downfall) was being preached among masses and had its evil effect on the university too. This university was destroyed by Muslim invaders and all its precious literature was burnt while the resident monks were slaughtered.

Takhshila or Texla University, located near the present day Rawalpindi in Pakistan, and in ruins today, was perhaps the oldest university in India. It had existed as a live institution for several thousand years. At the time of Alexander's invasion (329-325 BC), it was known as the greatest seat of learning all over Asia. Maharishi Patanjali, Chanakya[28] and Jeevaka[29] had been its students, and later, worked there as teachers too. Bhritya Kumar Ji, a well known surgeon, also was a teacher in the university. It is said that great scholars from foreign countries came here to study eighteen great subjects, chief of them being medicine, economics, politics, philosophy – especially Buddhist philosophy – literature, the four Vedas and sculpture. From 500 BC to the 6th century AD, Takhshila University was at the height of fame. During various excavations several objects have been found: brass utensils, pen, inkpot, diamond necklace, light posts, touchstone, antimony-container, statues of Kandhari art, and inscriptions in Brahmi and Kharashtri[30] alphabets which are seen in the museum of that place. The ruins cover several square miles. Besides, there is a pillar of King Kanishka who had lived and ruled several years before the birth of Christ. There are also ruins of the homes of Buddhist *Bhikshus*, their bathrooms etc. Several books on Hindu and Buddhist philosophy were written in this university. All these things throw a flood of light on the ancient Indian culture. This university was very big, bigger than Nalanda University. The age for admission into this University was sixteen years. Mostly sons of kings or of the aristocracy got admission into this university. Sons of poor people worked during the day and attended evening classes. Some of these students paid their fees later on. Special attention was paid towards social life and character development of students. This great university also was destroyed with the onset of the Muslim period.

Vikram Shila University was located at Sultan Ganj of modern Bhagalpur in Bihar. The university used to conduct a very strict entrance examination. The faculty consisted of 116 teachers. The Vedas, literature, philosophy and other subjects, including various arts, were taught in this university. There were hundreds of temples attached to this educational center. This university also was destroyed by Muslim invaders. Its buildings, along with its rich literature, and all temples in the vicinity were burnt. The invaders under the leadership of Mohammad Bin Bakhtiar killed King Govind Pall and looted and burnt both Nalanda University and Vikram Shila[31] University. Thousands of students and teachers, Indian and foreign, were massacred.

Dhan Katak University[32] was in the Deccan. It was also a big university. How it came to its end is not known.

Effects of foreign invasions on education, culture and social life in India

During the Renaissance Age which spanned the period circa 1000 BCE to 500 CE, or perhaps up to the beginning of the Rajput Period (600 CE to 1200 CE). This was followed by the Dark Age of India, replete with foreign invasions. India was at the zenith of prosperity and learning although the Renaissance movement had begun to disappear. Masses were taking full advantage of the educational opportunities provided in the country. Moreover, students came even from foreign countries for education. India's trade – both external and internal - was flourishing, and the agricultural production was very satisfactory too. India's navy had connected the subcontinent to the rest of Asia as well as with Egypt, Greece and Rome. India's culture had penetrated the whole of South East Asia, China, Burma, Ceylon, Manchuria, Mongolia, Japan and Pacific Islands, right up to the American continents. Shri Ganga Shankar Mishra, M.A., in his Hindi article *Sanskriti ki samasya* (The problem of Culture), published in the *Hindu Sanskriti Ank*, says: "In the east from Burma up to America in the west every country bears the stamp of ancient Indian culture on its own culture." He further quotes Mr. Kyujin as saying that in the languages of almost all these countries, the word for God seems to have been derived from the Sanskrit word Dev. Similarly, he further quotes Mr. King as saying in his book *Encyclopedia of Religion and Ethics Part7, Volume 2*, that in ancient Polynesian songs the *Vedic* ideology was clearly seen and by reading the thoughts of these people regarding heaven and hell, world and sky, this life and the next life, it looked as if *Vedic Mantras* were echoing from all these islands into the waters of the Pacific Ocean. Dr. Rendl has translated so many of these songs in his book *Polynesian Religion* to show how closely they resembled the Vedic ideology. Diwan Chaman Lal in his book *Hindu America* has shown how popular was Hindu culture in America. In western Asia in the countries of Afghanistan, Persia and Arabia and also in Egypt, there were so many scattered signs of Hindu culture. Ordinarily, Greece is thought to be the teacher of all Europe in philosophy and science. However, the flow of her philosophic and scientific thought also seems to be colored by the ancient principles of India's philosophy and metaphysics. Greece sent so many scholars like Pythagoras, Empedocles and Democritis etc to India for study. The ancient cultures of Scandinavia, Germany, Ireland and other countries of Europe have so much in common with the ancient culture of India. India had trade relations with Rome since very ancient times and this trade gradually fell into Muslim hands during the medieval times. In the sixteenth century there was again a direct contact between the western countries and India. The English, the French and the Dutch came to India for trade. During the Muslim rule in India, India's trade with the west came almost to a standstill and the study of ancient philosophy and spiritual science almost came to a close. The arts also bore the brunt of Muslim rule. Hindus stopped going to foreign countries during the period of Muslim domination. The medieval Indian history saw the decline and decay of indigenous empires and dynasties.

After Harsha[33] and Pulkeshi[34] their dominions were divided into several petty states. Thus small states replaced the bigger ones. The ruling kings, in their desire to appear as just towards all their sons, divided their kingdoms equally – sometimes even in their lifetimes – without looking into the evil effects of such a policy. They also did not know that dangerous times were ahead and that barbarous hordes in West Asia were about to fall upon the unprepared and divided India with a view to plunder, kill and convert them to Islam. These fragmentations of the country into small states made India weak militarily, politically as well as economically. Driven by petty jealousies these princely states often went to wars with each other for no substantive reason, becoming emaciated in the process. The solidarity of the country was lost. Solanki, Pal, Sen, Pratihara, Yadava, Guhil, Rathor and other dynasties were busy in their own petty quarrels.

As the *Vedic* and Epic times were quite peaceful and there was plenty of prosperity smiling on the whole land and there was hardly any impactful incident of foreign invasion, the idea of one strong central government was quite foreign to the Indian mind, especially when it was fully occupied with religious thought and practice during the Renaissance period. Of course there had been some great kings, who were empire builders too. Janmeja, Pushyamitra, Shung, Samudragupta, Chandra Gupta, Ashoka, Raja Bhoj, Rajaraja[35], Rajendra Chola etc, who conquered a large part of India while some of them conquered the whole of India and performed *Bajpeya Yajna*. There were others who conquered even some foreign lands and performed *Ashwamedh Yajna* (Horse worship/sacrifice) as celebration of their victories. But, generally, in her long history India, it seems, like most of the countries of the world in those times, was a country of small states. The small states in the medieval age gradually became demoralized and interstate wars set at naught all possibility of peace and progress in the country. The despotic princes thought less of the welfare of their subjects and more of their own glorification and luxury. The people had, now, no voice in the government as they used to before. Due to interstate wars every now and then the need for the army was felt more and more, necessitating more taxes on the people. The princes also began to appoint their ministers themselves – another departure from past practices. Thus they lost the love and sympathy of their subjects. The army also was not devoted to the state as before. As the princes spent more and more money on their own gratifications they could not keep good order in their states. They, therefore, became dependent upon mercenary soldiers recruited from other states and on untrained armies supplied by *Sardars*[36] and *Jagirdars*[37].

There was another canker-worm which had unfortunately entered into the body-politic of India after the *Mahabharata* War and was sapping the vitality of the nation. India had since long started on the road to ruin. She was gradually losing her national language, Sanskrit, which was a great unifying factor before. By losing Sanskrit the people lost touch with national literature which had an adverse impact upon the development of national character. Thus people were partitioned off into narrow compartments and became foreigners in their own country. By losing national common language and national literature they lost common interests and aims, common feelings and experiences, common customs and manners, common dress and their common ideology also lost much of its vigor; in the bargain the Indian civilization began to lose its inherent vitality and cohesiveness. It is my conviction that India's downfall dates from the period in which she lost her national language and national literature. After the country's division into petty states the memory of glorious past, comprising national history and culture – which were our precious heritage and great unifying factors – receded. This loss gave birth to a diversity of ideas and interests, attitudes and goals. Further, the sense of insecurity regarding life, honor and property, which had resulted from foreign invasions, cut down travel and communication to a great extent. Due to the absence of settled/stable and enduring government, dacoits and highwaymen infested the land. These factors encouraged regional insularity – and insularity among small principalities/kingdoms within regions – which generated and crystallized provincial dialects called *prakrit bhashas* and the deteriorated/corrupt forms of Sanskrit called *apbhranshas*. As with Muslims who spoke foreign language, people now were unable to understand Sanskrit and the literature in Sanskrit; there grew confusion in religious thought leading to cultural incoherence in the country. Several new religious groups came into being. India had already been politically divided into small and weak states; it was now further partitioned into numerous religious groups or communities – creating another source of weakness. People began to look upon their own petty state as their country and their own *prakrit* or *apbhransha* as their national language and their own small community within the borders of their state as their nation. Thus the great Indian people were fragmented into groups of small communities and India ceased to be a nation. The people of these states became narrow-minded, parochial, selfish and shortsighted. They forgot that India was one and indivisible, separated from the rest of the world by natural barriers and bound together as it was with common culture, common *Vedic* religion, common ideology, common customs and manners and way of life, common literature, common interests and common aims. The result was that when one state was overrun by foreign invaders very few among other states came to its help, if at all. When the next state came under the heel of the invader the rest of the states similarly thought that it was not their business to interfere and invite the wrath of the invader unnecessarily. Thus state after state was conquered and overrun and all their wealth was loaded on the camels, asses, horses and other means of transport and taken away as booty, along with thousands of selected and crying girls and women from all parts of the country. They were taken as slaves and marched on foot to distant lands where they were sold, it is said, for two rupees each. These invaders in some cases even exploited the religious susceptibilities of the people and kept a screen of cows in front of their advancing armies so that the Indian soldiers may not give battle for fear of injuring the cows; and their water resources were polluted with cows' blood to make them surrender. Thus the whole of India was conquered, plundered and enslaved. Some unfortunate people amongst us still, in some corners of the country, are victims to the same fell disease of the medieval times and are talking in terms of religion, province and provincial vernaculars. When will they wake up from their ignorance? If this dangerous disease is not checked in time, it may spell ruin on the country at anytime and the old history of invasions and long periods of slavery may be repeated.

It is a tragic irony that there was a time when India's cultural and spiritual riches, along with her well organized and widespread system of education used to attract foreign students and great scholars from Asia and Europe; while her material riches – the legendary wealth of her kings and business communities – and her political disunity held attraction for a different set of people, viz., hordes of rapacious adventurers and looters from the West, as well as from northwest Asia. Greeks invaded India in 327 BC under the leadership of Alexander the Great. But it had petered out on the subcontinent's borders itself for various reasons. Therefore, it left no enduring mark on the social and political life of India – whatever impact it might have had was perhaps absorbed into the Indian culture. Huns, Shakas[38] and other tribes that came to India were absorbed into the Hindu fold. However, not all aliens entered India as hostiles. For example, Christianity came to India within a few decades of the death of Christ and found India hospitable. Zoroastrians fled from Iran and found a safe haven in India. Judaism also sought and found safe haven in India. Islam also came to India within a few decades of the death of the Prophet and took roots in southern India peacefully. No section of Hindus opposed it. The Portuguese brought Catholicism to India towards the end of Middle Ages, it was not opposed by the locals on any grounds whatsoever – religious, ethnic or political.

Unfortunately, other Muslim invaders came, time and again, plundered the country and took away with them thousands of prisoners as slaves. Dara Gushtap, Mahmud Ghaznavi, Mohammad Gauri, Taimur, Sabkatgin, Babar, Nadir

Shah, Ahmad Shah Abdali etc. were some of the chiefs who led them. Mahmud Ghaznavi himself invaded India seventeen times. He sacked and plundered the famed Somnath Temple which contained several idols made of gold and silver, one of them fifteen feet high bedecked with diamonds. Near those idols there was a chain of gold weighing about one hundred mounds and carrying several bells. It is said that from that very temple Mahmud carried away booty to the tune of about one crore of rupees or more according to the standard of valuation of those times. In the same way he plundered the great temples of Mathura and Kannauj. It is said that in Kannauj alone ten thousand temples were plundered and destroyed. Almost every corner in the Kannauj of those times had a temple for worship.

Mohammad Gauri invaded India three times. In the first invasion he was defeated by Prithvi Raj Chauhan and fled. But Prithvi Raj's cousin Jai Chand, a great traitor, wrote a letter to Mohammad Gauri inviting him to come again and attack Prithvi Raj, offering to help him with his army against his own cousin. Muhammad Gauri returned and killed Prithvi Raj and went away with immense booty and prisoners. He invaded for the third time and this time he ransacked the state of Jai Chand, the black sheep. Jai Chand the traitor was killed and duly punished for his treason. (*Actually Gauri – either himself or through his lieutenants – had invaded India seven times. The author is referring to the two battles he had fought with Prithvi Raj Chauhan and one with Jai Chand. The details of his raids are as follows:*

The Conquest of Punjab and Sindh
In 1175, he attacked Multan and defeated the Ismailian Heretics, who were the ruling power there. Then, he conquered the fort of Uch. Later, he attacked Gujarat, but the powerful king Bhimdev defeated him. During 1179-1186 Gauri occupied Lahore and Sindh. With the help of the king of Jammu, he attacked Peshawar, and then occupied the fort of Sialkot.

The First Battle of Tarain
Mohammad Gauri moved towards Delhi in 1191 and occupied Sirhind. Thence he confronted Delhi's ruler, Prithvi Raj Chauhan at Tarain, a place about 10 miles from Karnal. The invader was routed.

The Second Battle of Tarain
Next year, Mohammad Gauri invaded India again, with 1,20,000 strong army comprising Afghans, Turks, and Persians etc. This time, aided by Jai Chand, Mohammad Gauri defeated and killed Prithvi Raj.

The Battle against Jai Chand
In 1194, Mohammad Gauri invaded India again and attacked Kannauj. In the battlefield of Chandawar, he defeated Jai Chand. Gauri appointed Qutub-ud-Din Aibak his viceroy and returned to Ghazni.

The Conquest of Gujarat and Bundelkhand
As viceroy of Mohammad Gauri, Qutub-ud-Din Aibak attacked Anhilwara, the capital of Gujarat. The king of Gujarat, Bhimdev, fought bravely and defeated Qutub-ud-Din, but the latter attacked again and this time he could defeat Bhimdev. Then he attacked Bundelkhand, which was under Chandel Rajputs. Qutub-ud-Din defeated them. 50,000 people were taken as prisoners. Mosques were constructed in place of the destroyed Hindu temples.

The Conquest of Bengal and Bihar
While Qutub-ud-Din was fighting in Gujarat and Bundelkhand, another slave of Mohammad Gauri, Mohammad-bin-Bakhtiyar Khilji, attacked Bihar in 1197. The Buddhist king of Bihar, Indraman, did not fight against the invaders. Without any battle, this state was occupied by Mohammad-bin-Bakhtiyar. The Buddhist-temples were destroyed and thousands of Buddhist monks were killed.

In 1202, Khilji attacked Bengal with a few soldiers. Lakshman Sen, the king, ran away. The invaders looted the state. Now, Khilji was the viceroy of Mohammad Gauri in Bengal and Bihar too.

The revolt of Khokhars

In 1205, Mohammad Gauri came to India, to crush the Khokhars' revolt. On March 15, 1206, when Gauri was going to Ghazni from Lahore, someone killed him in Dhamyak, district Jhelum, (now in Pakistan). It is said the murderer probably acted out of revenge for the massacres that Gauri had perpetrated on India.)[39]

Ahmad Shah Abdali invaded India six times, plundered the country and massacred millions of people, burnt towns and villages and took thousands of prisoners. The more heavily the camels were laden with the booty followed by long lines of prisoners, both male and female, the more tempting was the prospect of invading India for the barbarians from that part of Asia. How very shocking and humiliating was the whole spectacle! This plunder of India was a regular feature year after year and continued for one thousand years – even after the decline of the Mughal Empire had begun.

Foreign invasions and destruction of Indian States one after the other had devastating repercussions on the educational institutions, as also on the magnificent architectural efforts, the arts and industries, the rich literature, and on the culture as a whole. The invading hordes were cruel, barbarians and enemies of culture and civilization – riff-raffs of their own countries. They called themselves Muslim, but I wonder if they ever understood one word of the Quran. They were all converts at the point of the sword as most of the Muslims of those days were in Arabia, Persia, Turkey, Afghanistan, India, Egypt and South East Asia. They carried fire and sword wherever they went. They slaughtered people relentlessly. They pillaged towns and cities without compunction. They burnt to ashes big universities like Nalanda and Texla as well as innumerable other educational institutions. They desecrated, plundered and burnt as many holy temples as they could lay their hands upon, and built mosques in their place with the material taken out of the ruins of temples. The Parmara Raja Bhoj[40] had constructed at Bhojpur a very big artificial lake, considered to be the biggest in the world at that time, which fed several canals for irrigation purposes. This great lake was also destroyed by these ignorant people. The Victory Pillar of Dhar which was a beautiful piece of workmanship, a gem of Indian art, too was destroyed. Innumerable gems of architecture and other institutions, which had a halo of some historical or cultural importance about them, were razed to the ground.

Music was banned even by some of the Mughal Kings who had some taste for painting or architecture. They burnt precious Sanskrit settlements. There was no safety of life, of religious convictions, of honor and of property. *Purdah* and early marriage of girls came to India with Muslim invasions. According to Islam, it is said, carrying away of married women as slaves was forbidden. But, which of the Muslim invaders ever cared for the religious injunctions? For this reason, Hindus began to marry their daughters off even at the age of seven or eight and sometimes in their babyhood so that they might be safe. There were millions of forced conversions. Muslims who came to India from outside as invaders were only a few thousand in the beginning but they multiplied during the course of ten or twelve centuries. They took Hindu wives by force. There was a tradition, I do not know how far it was true, that the Mughal King Aurangzeb did not take his daily meals unless he had weighed in the balance a maund and a quarter of sacred threads (*Yagyopaveet*[41]) freshly taken from Hindu shoulders. It may be an exaggeration. But the blind zeal he had shown in this respect (forced conversions) cannot be doubted. However, even wholesale massacres of Hindus could not convert the whole of the country, as it had happened in other lands, in spite of the fact that Muslims ruled in this country for about a thousand years or so and Muslim Kings of India were the strongest in the world in those days. The strong cultural backbone of India proved itself more than a match for this blind religious fury and fanaticism. To exemplify the resistance to forced conversions the following instances should suffice: A small courageous boy like Haqiqat Rai, yet in his teens, could challenge a mighty government like the Mughal Empire. He smilingly kissed the sword with which he was to be beheaded but refused to be converted to Islam. The brave sons of Guru Gobind Singh, not yet in their teens, also refused to purchase their lives and liberty by selling their religious convictions and this country's honor. Both of them preferred to be buried alive in a mosque's wall at Sirhind town (the town's name means the heads of Hindus – to commemorate that brutal and heinous crime. This new name was given to the town, it appears, after that great sacrifice on the altar of Mother India's great culture).

To protect their chastity against the wicked invaders Queen Padmini[42] and her fourteen thousand (or twenty four thousand, according to some sources) lady companions jumped into burning pyres in Chittor and perished even as their men-folk were engaged in life and death struggle in the battlefield. Similarly, Maharana Pratap Singh, Durga Das Rathor, Chattarpati Shivaji, Guru Teg Bahadur, Guru Gobind Singh, Banda Bahadur et al underwent untold ordeals but did not bow their heads before the detestable inhuman culture of the invaders. Indian culture has produced men like Brahmchari Tapasvi Arjuna who did not allow himself to be captivated by the unparalleled beauty of Urvashi and addressed her as mother; men like Maharana Pratap and Rathor Durga Dass returned respectively to their husbands the Begums, wives of Muslim kings, after they had been captured in war. Though a few million people, with somewhat weaker minds, fell prey to the logic of the sword India be proud of the fact that the majority of her children remain the torch bearers of her ancient unique culture, with their religious convictions intact.

However, the Indian education suffered immensely in the midst of religious persecutions for thousand long years that generated panic, fear and frustration. Sometimes it would appear to be working normally, but often faced suppression. For want of state patronage and due to the panicky conditions of the times the educational system gradually lost much of its charm, efficiency and completeness. The teaching of all spiritual as well as academic knowledge and of arts and crafts suffered a very serious setback till it nearly vanished. The only education that was left was of the extremely poor moral or literary quality which aimed at liberalizing one's mind and outlook on the world to some extent.

Islamic Education

Muslim Kings were no patrons of education. Thus, in spite of the fact that Mughal Kings were powerful, had a big empire and vast sources of income they did not put in place an efficient educational system. The Islamic teaching was carried on in some small schools or in mosques. It was of literary or theological variety, consisting of memorizing some poems of unrequited love, ballads and love stories; then there were madrasas where young Muslims studied Quran. The pendulum like motion of the head indicated the great effort demanded of the reader of Quran as it was unintelligible, being in a foreign (Arabic) tongue. As Professors D. Moudgil and O. Banerjee say in their *Recurrent Essays*: "Except imparting instruction in literary subjects and scriptural law, few teachers taught anything and none labored on scientific and material aspects of life. 'Preparation for complete living' was thus distinctly absent from the curricula of instruction. It was not without its effects. Either it led to the birth of fanaticism and egotistical bigotry or too vague liberalism. Either a Changez Khan or a Chaitanya, in either case too inadequate to give life a constructive handling."

III. The Pre-British System of Education as carried on by Indian People themselves

After the downfall of the Mughal Empire people started organizing education again – mostly in the form of individual initiatives. According to Lala Lajpat Rai's book *Unhappy India*, "We had our own indigenous popular system of education before the British came". There were Brahamanic, Buddhist and Muslim schools all over the country. "Side by side, however, with these", says Rev. Kecy[43], "there grew up at the same time, in most parts of India, a popular system of elementary education which was open generally to all comers. It must have arisen to supply a popular demand for instruction in reading, writing and arithmetic and was made use of chiefly by the trading and agricultural classes.

"Few countries and certainly no western ones" continues Rev. Kecy, "have had systems of education with such a long and continuous history with so few modifications as some of the educational systems of India. The long centuries through which they have held sway show that they must have possessed elements which were of value and that they were not unsuited to the needs of those who developed and adopted them. They produced many great men and earnest seekers after truth and their output on the intellectual side is by no means inconsiderable. They developed many noble educational ideals which are a valuable contribution to educational thought and practice." Widespread indigenous system of education and how it worked is fully described by Dr. Leitner in his *History of Indigenous Education in the Punjab*, says Lajpat Rai. Leitner was the first Principal of the Lahore Government College and, later on, the Director of Public Instruction, Punjab.

Lajpat Rai goes on to add, "The indigenous system of elementary education was bound up with the Indian village system (Headman, accountant, police officer, priest and school master)". Mr. Ludlow, quoted by Lajpat Rai, says: "In every Hindu village which has retained anything of its form ... the rudiments of knowledge are sought to be imparted, there is not a child except those of the outcastes (who form no part of the community) who is not able to read, to write, to cipher, in the last branch of learning they are confessedly most proficient..."

"Where the village system has been swept away by us as in Bengal there the village school has equally disappeared" says Mr. Ludlow in *British India*, quoted by Dr. Leitner[44], page 18.

According to Mr. A.P. Howell in his book *Education in British India prior to 1854 and in 1870-71* and quoted by Lala Lajpat Rai in his book *Unhappy India*, "In Bengal alone in 1835 Mr. Adam estimated their (indigenous schools') number to be 100,000; in Madras, upon an enquiry instituted by Sir Thomas Munro in 1822, the number of schools was reported to be 12,498 containing 1,88,650 scholars and in Bombay, about the same period, schools of a similar order were found to be scattered all over the Presidency...."

Dr. Leitner further says, "Just as the introduction of specimens of the art industry of India has tended largely to develop the present artistic taste among English workmen, so did the methods of instruction pursued in indigenous schools influence the schools in England."

Dr. Leitner, on page 3 of his report, says, "In backward districts like that of Hoshiarpur the Settlement Report of 1852 shows a school to every 19.65 male inhabitants (adults and non-adults) which may be contrasted with the present proportion of one Government or Aided School to every 2818.7 inhabitants." (During the British regime).

Figures about Punjab as given by Dr. Leitner in 1854:- "3,33,550 persons attended schools. The school leaving figure for indigenous secular schools and schools in private houses of teachers, according to the last census, was 1,57,623."

According to Dr. Leitner, "There were so many girls' schools in the Punjab before the annexation by the British... Six Public Schools for girls were kept by Punjabi women at Delhi alone and these women had emigrated to the south for this purpose... Among Mohammedans very many widows considered it a sacred duty to teach girls to read the Quran and though Delhi, like the rest of the N.W. Province, was far behind the Punjab in female education, we find that it had, in 1845, numerous schools for girls kept in private houses... The British occupation was actually followed by decline in women's education. The causes were: Urdu took the place of Punjabi, weakening of the religious feeling, spread of adultery under British regime causing jealousy to the male sex in granting much liberty to the female sex, bad tone of the education, too much interference by the State in girl schools, and their location at public places."

The arrival of European nations in India

It was quite evident that the fame of India's wealth and prosperity had long reached Europe during the Medieval Age through Indian trade. But the Mughal Kings were very powerful in those days and no European nation could think of attempting to seize by force the political power from them. Thus the European infiltration was considerably delayed. Although the interaction between Europeans and the Mughal Court had begun – it was still at perfunctory levels involving such stray cases as Thomas Roe treating Jahangir's daughter and, as reward, getting some trade concessions for his country from the Emperor.

After some time, when the downfall of the Mughal Empire became sufficiently discernible, European countries began to cherish dreams of possessing India and her coveted wealth. They knew that the Muslim political power was crumbling; the people also were weak and divided; the long-lasting slavery under foreign kings had deprived them of national character. Ambitious and enterprising people of some European countries like Vasco-Da-Gama, Columbus, Diaz and several others, encouraged by their kings, started on their air-driven ships in quest of India – although the initial quest was trade and commerce it became a full-fledged colonial ambition later on when India's political climate appeared to be conducive to such adventures. Some of the voyagers, instead of reaching India, found the American continent and other islands. On stepping onto the shores of America they came across the inhabitants and called them Indians and subsequently Red Indians when they discovered that it was some other country and not India, so obsessed they were in their search for India. They came to some other islands and named them West Indies; the dream about India had captivated their minds to such an extent that when the Dutch, instead of reaching India, passed much further south and went eastward and found a group of islands they named them as East Indies.

However, the Portuguese were successful in reaching India followed by the English and the French. The Portuguese were content to settle in certain small colonies on the western coast. But the English and the French had bigger ambitions – they wanted to eventually build Empires *a la* the Mughals. Moreover, they were fighting against each other in Europe, which intensified their struggle for supremacy in the subcontinent.

The English were successful in besting the French who were subsequently content to have some small strips of territories on the coasts of India[45]. The English, more ambitious and resourceful of the two, began to conquer parts of India bit by bit using trickery, fraud and blackmail aided by Indian mercenary soldiers and bankrolled by petty *rajas* and *nawabs*. They were adept at setting one state against the other. They sometimes sided with one prince and sometimes with another and grabbed some part of the territory by way of reward for their assistance and guidance. Thus a great part of India was conquered by Indian mercenary soldiers themselves and handed over to their British masters. Could the pathetic degeneration and demoralization of the Indians of those days have gone further than this? About a third part of the country, called Princely India, was still left with some of the influential and historically or dynastically important princes for political reasons. Since the British East India Company had not become well entrenched yet, these States were not annexed but used as tributaries; these vassal-states were used to serve as buffers against any future political reactions or even aspirations of the people of the conquered territories. Over a period of time they realized that Hindus, constituting the majority and politically alive community, could not be kept enslaved perpetually.

After occupying the country, the conquerors had to take up the task of consolidating their power. At that time the standard of Indian education was very low. Since the Muslim rulers, especially the Mughals, took no interest in education and the people – suppressed for centuries, with their social institutions destroyed – were left to their own devices. There, however, had come about at that time a system of popular education which was integrated with the village system comprising one headman, one accountant, one priest, one police officer and one teacher.

Although the teaching was of elementary type, (in sharp contrast with the *Gurukula* System of the *Vedic* or the Epic Age or the great universities of the *Sutra* Age), limited to the 3 R's (Reading, wRiting and aRithmetic) still it was unbearable to the British foreign government. They thought that the indigenous education, if allowed to flourish, may regenerate enlightenment, self-respect and ultimately a desire for political emancipation. The conquerors, therefore, first thought of stopping all education by destroying the village system of the country. The village system was considered to be a part of the body politic of India[46]. But, subsequently, they decided to introduce a certain type of education which, on the one hand, consolidated and perpetuated their rule and, on the other, tended to further demoralize the people – making them lose all sense of nationhood. In the process it would churn out a class of abject dependants and hirelings who would cooperate with the conquerors in consolidating the alien rule. Thus an education policy built on such political motive was framed, after a hot debate in the British Parliament, under the leadership of Lord Macaulay. Indians fell an easy prey to this conspiracy as they wanted some sort of education for their children especially when they had no, or meager, resources to run schools of their own and possessed no means of giving a united resistance to the foreign power. They were all the more despairing as they had already seen a thousand years of slavery, misrule and anarchy of the worst type during the alien Muslim reign. Observed Professor E.A. Ross, as quoted by Lajpat Rai in his *Unhappy India,* "Subjection to a foreign yoke is one of the most potent causes of the decay of nations"; and in this way the long drawn out slavery of the Muslim period had considerably weakened and demoralized the Indian people and they could not raise voice in the beginning against the new educational policy. Thus, India fell from the frying pan into the fire. This is what happens to countries that are conquered by a foreign nation. This is what the Romans did in Britain, the British did in Ireland, in India and in all British possessions, the Chinese in Japan, the Japanese in China, the Americans in Hawaii and Cuba, and Germany in Poland after carrying out territorial conquests at different times. The first thing a conqueror does after the military conquest of a nation is to mold the educational system, the schools and universities. Thereafter, he sets about preparing the 'history' that discourages and disparages its people – a caricature of its true history, distorting the events and showing in prominence its defeats, failures and internal divisions/disagreements/contradictions.

Thus, proving in every manner that it deserves neither independence nor progress. It becomes necessary for the occupying force/imperial power to have pliant people from amongst the conquered, who have some pretense to intelligence and education, and can be persuaded to play the second fiddle to the alien masters in the domain of education. The imperial power organizes this clique in the form of a Text Book Committee and asks the members of this body, in exchange for a tempting salary or offer of some high post in the administration, to write books which may further demoralize the children of the conquered nation, which may give them wrong ideals and wrong facts of history, thus turning them into inert dependants of the alien rule. The conqueror does not write these school textbooks himself, lest it should create suspicion in the minds of the people and trigger off mass resentment. In this manner lackeys become handy in perpetuating an education system that emasculates an entire nation.

The British educational policy in India

The British Educational Policy and its how and why may better be stated in the words of Britain's own administrators and thinkers: (as mentioned in Hardayal's *Thoughts on Education* and Lajpat Rai's *Unhappy India*). Macaulay says, (Macaulay's *Minute on Education* of 1835), "We must at present do our best to form a class who may be interpreters between us and the millions we govern; a class of persons Indian in blood and color, but English in taste, in opinion, in morals and in intellect."

Charles Grant, in his book, *The Education of the Indian People*, published towards the end of the 18th century, observes, "On success (of the new educational policy) would be our safety, not our danger. We shall take the most rational means to remove inherent great disorders, to attach the Hindu people to ourselves, to ensure the safety of our possessions, to enhance continually their value to us." He further goes on to say: "(We want) to attach our subjects by affection, by interest, by winning them to our religion and our sentiments". That, in his opinion, "would have the effect of rendering our authority permanent and secure."

Sir William W. Hunter, in his book, *The Indian Mussallmans*, published in 1871, elucidated a general principle in these words: "The chronic peril which environs British power in India is the gap between the Rulers and the Ruled. The educational system helps British influence by bridging the gulf between the white and the brown and breaking down the barriers which Hindu exclusiveness had erected between aggressive conquerors of various races and creeds and the weak and divided and spiritless Hindu community."

Rev. Alexander Duff, the father of Christian education in India and pioneer of English education in Bengal, in his paper, *An Exposition of the late Governor General of India's Last Act,* says: "When the Romans conquered a province they forthwith set themselves to the task of Romanising it, that is, they strove to create a taste for their own more refined language and literature and thereby aimed at turning the song and the romance and the history, the thought and the feeling and the fancy of the subjugated people into Roman channels which fed and augmented Roman interests. And has Rome not succeeded?"

Sir Alexander Arbuthnot K.C.S.I, a member of the Supreme Council of India, remarked in the course of his address he delivered to the students of the Calcutta University in 1880, "My conviction is that the more thorough and the more complete the education is which we impart to the people of India, the better fitted they will be to appreciate the blessings of British rule and they will depreciate any material change in the existing order of things."

Sir Richard Temple Bart, in his well known book, *India in 1880*, says, "Of late, certain symptoms of disloyalty manifested by some limited sections of certain educated classes have caused reflections to be made against the effects of education upon native loyalty. But that disloyalty was traceable to social and traditional circumstances quite apart from educational causes and was checked, not fostered or encouraged by education. There doubtless will be found disloyal individuals among the educated classes as there are among all classes in a country subjected to foreign rule. Nevertheless, a well-founded assurance may be entertained that those natives who have learnt to think through the medium of the language and are imbued with the literature and the philosophy of England will bear towards the English nation that heartfelt allegiance which men may feel without at all relinquishing their own nationality."

Sir C. Trevelyan, a relative of Lord Macaulay, who served John Company in various capacities and rose to be the Governor of Madras and Member of the Supreme Council in India, says in his book, *On the Education of the People of India*, "In following this course (of spending a million sterling annually on education) we should be trying no new experiment. The Romans at once civilized the natives of Europe and attached them to their rule by Romanizing them or in other words by educating them in the Roman literature and arts and teaching them to emulate their conquerors instead of opposing them. Acquisitions made by superiority in war were consolidated by superiority in the arts of peace and the remembrance of the original violence was best in that of the benefits which resulted from it. The provincials of Italy, Spain, Africa and Gaul (old name for France) having shared their privileges with them remained to the last faithful subjects of the Empire and the union was at last dissolved not by internal revolt but by the shock of external violence which involved conquerors and conquered in one common overthrow. The Indians will, I hope, soon stand in the same position towards us in which we once stood towards the Romans. Tacitus[47] informs us that it was in the policy of Julius Agricola[48] to instruct the sons of leading men among the Britons in the literature and science of Rome and to give them a taste for the refinement of Roman civilization. We all know how well this plan answered.

From being obstinate enemies the Britons soon became attached and confiding friends and they made more strenuous efforts to retain the Romans then than their ancestors had done to resist their invasions." He further argued that the indigenous education would not make for the safety of the British Raj. He, therefore, wanted Indian youth to be nurtured on English education. He says further, "The spirit of English literature cannot but be favorable to the English connection. Similarly acquainted with us by means of our literature, the Indian youth will almost cease to regard us as foreigners... From violent opponents they are converted into zealous and intelligent cooperators with us." Returning to our young men brought up at our seminaries, he further goes on, "Instead of regarding us with dislike, they court our society and look upon us as their natural protectors and benefactors, the summit of their ambition is to resemble us."

Lord Mayo in his address at Calcutta University in 1869 said, "I am not without hope that perhaps in the establishment of the school, the college and the University, we may be weaving a golden land which may bind in closer union the subjects of our queen, be they dark or fair whether they reside in the east or the west."

From the above lengthy quotations of the British administrators themselves it would be crystal clear how demoralizing has been the effect of the Britain-imposed system of education on our youth. Some of the far-seeing people among our intelligentsia, with a view to save our young men from the demoralization de-spiritualization and de-nationalization, to which they were subjected in the Government schools, tried to open some national institutions for them.

History of the Movement for National Education: Reaction to the evils of the British education policy in India

With the aim of providing modern education while keeping the Indian values intact, the Dayanand Anglo Vedic College was set up at Lahore. Similarly, several educational institutions came into being, viz., the Banaras College, the Aligarh College, the Gurukula Academy at Hardwar, the Ferguson College at Poona and the Tagore School at Bolpur (Bengal). The abovementioned colleges also had highly developed schools running under their guidance.

However, there remained doubts about how authentic their claims to being national educational institutions were. After all, these had to work under a colonial regime and could not possibly be openly subversive or nationalistic. Moreover, since their financial condition was not exactly in the pink, these institutions had to submit to the governmental control. As stated by Lajpat Rai in his book, *The Problem of National Education in India*, "all models in the spirit of national education, in the form of D.A.V. College, Banaras College, Aligarh College failed due to the Government aid accepted by them which brought Government control in its train." The Government control brought with it the uniformity of syllabi, of the teaching methods and of the aims and objects of education with the Government institutions. Thus, the very aim for which these national institutions were brought into being was lost. There was another evil that was born with these institutions. They had a narrow sectarian outlook and, therefore, could not be called truly national in character. In the initiation of these institutions, as they did a lot of religious propaganda against other religious denominations, several other institutions representing other religious sects came into being. After some years there was not a single religious community in the whole of Punjab which did not have a school or college of its own. All these institutions cared less for education and more for propaganda and publicity of its connected religion. The result was that they indoctrinated bigotry and religious fanaticism among our young men and women, which cut at the very root of true education and, therefore, stymied the formation of national identity. This turned Punjab into a hotbed of reaction, intrigue and communal mischief. This situation was very favorable to the Imperial interests. Therefore, the alien government further fanned this fire of religious fanaticism turning it into flames of sectarian hatred and, in the process, injecting the poison of communalization into the education system of Punjab which gradually spread throughout the body politic, thus considerably delaying the dawn of political freedom in India. Effects of this poison can still be seen in some parts of the country in the form of a few selfish miscreants who are in the habit of taking up the cause of certain religious communities, provincial vernaculars or territorial boundaries. The truth however is that the bad education which they have got in these communal institutions has made them extremely selfish, greedy, bigoted and, in the process, thoroughly demoralized and denationalized. While they crave for Government jobs and positions they pretend to be guardians and protectors of their respective communities, states and vernaculars. They nurture the desire to further subdivide the country into smaller states and thus to promote their own personal interests so that they may have better opportunities for high positions in the newly created states.

The Gurukula Academy at Hardwar (Uttar Pradesh) was founded, managed, staffed and financed by Indians themselves. The medium of instruction in the Academy was Hindi and the study of Sanskrit was considered important. Coeducation was not entertained and teaching of fine arts was neglected.

Spartan in outlook, it encouraged the students to lead simple and abstemious life and follow the routine of early rising, bath, physical exercise, praying and performing *homa*[49] or sacrificial rites as well as observing *Brahmcharya* till the age of 24. The Academy was entirely independent of government control. It had its own courses of study without any interference from a government owned university. It enforced the ancient *Gurukula* discipline among its pupils. It, however, fell short of the mark and its progress was greatly retarded due to paucity of funds for want of State patronage; as a natural consequence of its independent stance the doors to Government service were already closed to the graduates from this institution. There was no other career opening for them as all indigenous industry in the country had been ruthlessly crushed by the foreign power in order to promote and protect British commercial interests. The only avenue of employment left for the Gurukula Academy's graduates was, perhaps, priesthood. But how many priests could be accommodated in the country in those days? The Gurukula Academy further failed for want of a countrywide public support as it was, after all, a sectarian institution.

The Shanti Niketan School at Bolpur, founded by Gurudev Rabindra Nath Tagore in 1901, about 100 miles north of Calcutta, was initially a one man institution. Its curriculum also was not sufficiently broad-based in the beginning. In 1921, however, it was officially established as University called *Vishva Bharti* – taken from the *Vedic* text which means "Where the whole world forms one single nest"[50]. It is a residential and coeducational institution that prefers the canopy of heaven i.e. it has open-air classes. It prepares students for the various examinations (up to B.A. level) of Calcutta University. Thus most of the evils of the British imposed system are sure to creep in by way of teaching methods, curricula and objectives although it has several departments now, viz., *Vidya Bhawan* (School of Research), *Shiksha Bhawan* (College), *Patha Bhawan* (School), *Kala Bhawan* (School of fine arts and crafts), *Sangit Bhawan* (School of music and dancing), *Sriniketan* (Institute of rural reconstruction), *Silpa Bhawan* (School of Industries), *Cheena Bhawan*, *Hindi Bhawan*, the *Islamia Research Section* and so on. There is also provision for painting, sculpture, etching (engraving) and wood carving. There are two degrees, viz., *Sanatak* (graduate) and *Vachaspati* (Doctorate degree). Although the ideals it represents are excellent it has no place for higher education of the modern type which India needs.

The Ferguson College at Poona is similarly an institution which cannot be called truly national.

"The only effort of national education" says Lajpat Rai in his book, *The Problem of National Education in India*, "was made by the National Council of Education in Bengal under the impetus of *Swadeshi* movement and the boycott of British goods" in the days when the whole of Bengal – rather the whole of India – was up in arms over the partition of Bengal during the viceroyalty of Lord Curzon. "The Scheme of the National Council was free from the sectarian evil of the upper India movements and took ample cognizance of the economic needs of the country as a whole and frankly recognized the necessity of ignoring the official university curricula and State aid. It aimed at national consolidation and national independence." As it was a direct challenge to the government it failed as it came into conflict with the resourceful government. Even its leaders fell prey to the frowns of the government and gave it a death blow themselves.

Thus, none of the abovementioned institutions – no matter how impressive its curriculum was – could make any substantial contribution towards providing solution to the problem of national education. Without political emancipation the solution of this problem was clearly not possible. Thus India was caught in a vicious circle. Without political power education could not be nationalized; and with the increasing deterioration of education's quality in the hands of the foreign government, and due to communal poisoning, the attainment of political power was a mere dream.

IV. The British-imposed system of education: Why it should go

Education Policy in India discussed in the British Parliament.

When the country was in the throes of political, nonviolent revolution, things were allowed to drift in the educational field. People were unable to change the government's education policy or have any reforms introduced in the curricula. The common people and well-meaning leaders, therefore, had to perforce wait for the day of their political deliverance. Several great thinkers and educationists of India published their views on the British-imposed system of education. Some of them like Lala Hardayal, Lala Lajpat Rai, Dr. Annie Besant and P.M. Mehta, at different periods of time, had launched crusades against the British education policy. A glance through their views on the subject may be of some interest even today.

According to the late Hardayal the British educational policy in India was killing the very soul of the Indian nation from the intellectual, moral and social points of view. It was crushing the conscience of India's middle and upper classes. He further noted that after conquering India, Britain consolidated its power by establishing its own schools and colleges that induced demoralization and denationalization among the successive generations of Indians. It further consolidated its power by taking Indians into the civil administration in order to develop common interest with intelligent and influential sections of the people. This would not only keep them away from assuming the role of leaders of their compatriots in the opposition but also curb the fighting spirit of the masses against foreign domination. Gradually the people of India would forget the pangs of conquest and be tamed under the policy of conciliation. They thought that with the policy of conciliation, they would slowly acquire social superiority over the conquered people. Victory in the battlefield had given them military and political supremacy over the Indian people, but the acceptance of offices in the administration by the influential sections of the subject populace would give the British an important and superior position in the social system of the country and also gain general credibility and acceptance. The lower strata could also be kept busy in hankering after, or by employing them in, cheap jobs in the administration. This "system of sweating" at the bottom could be further utilized in justifying and interpreting all moves of the foreign government as being for the benefit of the common subjugated people and thus be used as a safe medium to carry out all schemes with which the British Government representatives would not like to directly associate themselves. Thus a class comprising greedy, hypocritical, unscrupulous, cowardly, cunning, cringing and characterless government servants would be created all over the country which would serve as a sound bulwark against all attempts/ideas of rebellion as the vested interests of these purchased slaves would be intertwined with those of the foreign exploiters.

Again, both the British Education Policy in India and the Policy of Conciliation were useful tools in the expansion of British commerce as these facilitated social and intellectual conquest of India. The political and military conquest only destroys the organized physical strength of a subject nation, but the social and intellectual conquest emasculates the very core of its social life and destroys its national genius, not to mention its distinct identity. The ingredients that go into the foundations of a nation are its creative powers as expressed through its culture, language, literature, heritage and history. These we inherit from the past. Unfortunately, these have been vitiated, mutilated and thrown out of gear by the conquerors. This has resulted in reduced, if not nil, chances for building a vibrant national superstructure in the future, by structuring a national education system according to the needs of a sovereign nation.

Our national language, Sanskrit, had been disrupted by the *Mahabharata* war as explained elsewhere in this book. It was killed by foreign Muslim invasions, while its corpse was thrown out to rot by the British. It is true that the latter did not uproot our provincial dialects or *apbhranshas*, i.e., the mixture of Hindi & Sanskrit languages with foreign tongues. They did not crush them not for our benefit but for the sake of their own imperial interests. They knew that the foolish babble will keep us permanently divided in the form of linguistic and regional communities, thus preventing the formation of a united Indian nation, and thus perpetuating their domination.

Mr. Sidney Brooks, as quoted by Lala Hardayal, in his book *New Ireland*, observes "The British Education System all but destroyed the Gallic language which is now confined to the suburbs but which was universally spoken in Ireland a hundred years ago. The Irish language was injured if not actually paralyzed in the foreign system..." America also, adds Hardayal, "Americanized her new subjects in Asia and Australia... The Americans granted "concessions" to Cubans and Hawaiians of their own free will immediately after the conquest. The American government even supplies the text books free of charge in Cuba! Thus the Islanders are being civilized. Poles (people of Poland) resisted Germany while she imposed German language (on them to denationalize them)."

Strangely, our people would stick to English language with a tenacity that would never relax its hold on them under various pretexts, especially that it is a language universally understood. Then why don't the Germans, the French, the Russians and other nations of Europe adopt it and discard their own languages? Sometimes they say higher education will suffer for want of suitable technical terms and books in science and technology. Then they say that it was English language and English education which gave political unity to India. It is a partial truth at best. Unity – political or otherwise – of India was never on the agenda of the British rulers. It was in fact our grievances, disabilities and sufferings that gave birth to this unity. Who are these disrupters of Indian unity if not some of the English educated people, who would sell India off if they could find a suitable buyer?

We are a fine lot. We want to build a magnificent edifice of India with finely polished, nicely baked bricks without using the cement mixture to keep them together. How long will it stand in this manner? It will crumble faster than we can imagine, creating in the process a balkanized subcontinent with limited regional economies, with real and imaginary disputes exploding into internecine wars over border encroachments, air space, railway systems, land and water resources etc, eventually attracting foreign invasions. The only sensible way to resolve the lingual confusion was not the distribution of States on lingual basis out of fear of fasts-unto-death undertaken by various chauvinists, but a strong Home Policy reinforced by the Law of High Treason against all this treasonable conduct and to twist the tail of lingual hooligans with a strong iron grip and not to run away from this important issue in a cowardly manner. The policy could have been formulated in a rational manner to save India from the ultimate ruin that is awaiting us if we stick to our present way of looking at things. Lala Hardayal has rightly said "Language is a brand of society. It marks off our countrymen from the strangers." We call it mother tongue because, without it, we cannot exist even for a day. Our true national language for millennia has been Sanskrit, which has also been the repository of all our greatness and wisdom accumulated over the ages. Hindi is the main gateway through which we have to reach Sanskrit and our great treasure house of spiritual wisdom and even material glory by gradually sanskritizing Hindi after each decade and in ten jumps and by a progressive bilingual medium of education in all States. Carlyle once wrote that if he were asked to give up the Indian Empire and Shakespeare he would gladly forgo the former and not the national poet of England. The Empire, he said, must go some day but Shakespeare represented the eternal, imperishable wealth of England...

Hardayal further says, "Sanskrit literature must lose ground before English if the present system endures. Our society draws its morality and religion, its social spirit and its laws from the *Shastras*. The decline of Sanskrit learning will deprive us of national institutions.

"Ayurveda is being undermined by Government Medical Colleges. A Hindu young man can become a graduate in Philosophy without reading anything of Hindu metaphysics, the highest product of Hindu genius...."

"The British Education System will destroy Sanskrit literature and learning which is the pride and glory of our race and the wellspring of our moral and social ideals... With literature will go our culture and arts."

Shri Hardayal stresses the importance of national history: "What *Upanishads* are to the individual soul, History is to the collective organization called a nation. It is the means of self-realization and emancipation...

"National history is the *sine qua non* of national unity and growth. A nation that has no past must lack cohesion and patriotism. Common hero-worship is the bond of society. .... A common historical background is one of the indispensable conditions of national growth. Common political ideals and aspirations are impossible without a common past.

"The British rulers of India teach our boys what is really a caricature of Hindu history. The text books written by the

Lethbridges[51] and Hunters[52] of the Anglo-Indian community give us no idea of our ancient great men. They impress on the minds of our boys the notion that we have been an incapable race since the dawn of history and that our only function has been to lose battles one after another in the course of centuries. There is no mention of all that should be the pride of every Hindu.

"Woe to the nation that allows its children to read history as it is written by its foreign conqueror. No people with a particle of self-respect would tolerate it even for a moment. We may be unable to emulate our ancestors but let us at least refrain from reviling them.

"A man who sends his son to an Anglo-Indian School commits the sin of *pitri ninda* (reviling one's ancestors), the vilification of national heroes, dishonoring of national history."

It is the result of such mischievous histories written as a command performance of the British Government of India that all our so-called educated people, not excepting even our great leaders, are misguided in some very important facts of the Indian history. The stamp of the insidiously slanted history on their brain during the years of school age has been strong and tyrannical. The mischief of such historians needs to be fully exposed and countered.

According to Hardayal the British system of education in India and the British colonial rule tried to disrupt India's social system and throw it out of gear. It upset all rules and conventions of the Hindu Varan ashram – which with all its defects (correctable) is perhaps, till date, the most rational division of labor on such a mass scale. The British system made a *Brahman* redundant in Indian social life by taking upon itself the work of teacher. It made *Kshatriya* irrelevant by placing the defense of the country into the hands of a foreign power of occupation. It made *Vaishya* unnecessary by destroying all Indian Industry and thus increasing the population pressure on land. It hurt the *Sudra* also by putting an end to all indigenous industry and by making government service the only goal of life by equipping him with defective education and paying poor wages due to severe competition. The entire structured national life was thus thrown off its hinges. The Muslim invaders gave it the first shock from which it had not yet recovered when the British power stepped into the shoes of Mughal emperors and completed India's social ruin.

This system of education, according to Hardayal, de-Hinduized the young men of India and demoralized and denationalized them. For our young men schools and colleges were no better than comfortable prisons where truth was stabbed and patriotism was penalized and confidence was strangulated. According to Mr. Gokhale, Mr. Ranade once wrote an essay deprecating the British system of government in comparison with the Maratha rule. Sir Alexander Grant, the Principal of Elphinstone College, Bombay, who had great admiration for Mr. Ranade's talents, sent for him and after pointing out to him the error of his views, advised him, 'Young man you should not thus run down a government which is educating you and doing so much for your people.' And to mark his serious displeasure he suspended Mr. Ranade's scholarship for six months.

Lala Hardayal further quotes Sir W. Lee Warner who in his little book, *The citizen of India*, teaches our boys the following precious truth, "There is no drain of wealth from India to England. The former rulers of India never cared for the people. India is growing in prosperity under British rule." Sir W. Lee Warner's knowledge of the Indian history might have extended only up to Muslim invaders. The much talked of prosperity of India culminated in bringing per capita income of an Indian to six pies per day!

Finally, Mr. Hardayal points to the heavy strain on our school and college students caused by the artificial method of teaching through the medium of English which undermined the health of Indian nation in the long run.

Mr. Hardayal did not touch, however, the constructive side of the problem of Indian education. It was perhaps too early to do so, as India was groaning under heavy chains of slavery at that time and was concentrating all her energies towards political emancipation first.

What a pity that there are people amongst us even now who still cherish English language and cling to it all the time under various pretexts even after India has freed herself from English rule. They cling to it as a demoralized slave without self-respect would hug the heavy chains shackling him without feeling their weight or the disgrace of holding them.

"As to the other virtues which have adorned Hindu character from time immemorial, viz., simplicity, temperance, courtesy, family affection and respect for elders, the British educational system is notoriously fatal to their development."

Lala Lajpat Rai was one of the four top ranking patriots and political leaders India had produced during the 19th and 20th centuries. He was a brave and fearless patriot, a dynamic personality, a great statesman and a man with vision whose thundering voice made the alien power quake. He was known as the "Lion of the Punjab". He was in fact the Lion of India. He spent several years in jail for India's freedom. He was deported to Burma and kept there as a prisoner in the Mandalay Fort for some years where the Mughal King Shah Alam had been kept. Before being deported to Mandalay, I remember that he was arrested on one quiet evening and his bungalow at Lahore was surrounded with machine guns, and the whole of the white population at Lahore slept for the night at the Lahore Railway Station with special trains ready to take them to a place of safety if need be. Although his arrest was kept a secret the news spread like wild fire during the night throughout the length and breadth of the country. As he was being taken in a special train to Calcutta, people in the morning lay on the railway lines in thousands to stop the special train even by risking their lives. The train, therefore, took to the other unknown route and he was taken via Madras to Burma. He finally died in 1928 as a martyr to the sacred cause of India's independence when he, while advocating the boycott of Simon Commission, fell to *lathi* blows from a British official. Several newspapers sported black borders as sign of mourning, and included in the day's editions only one news item pertaining to his death and various condolence meetings and processions in almost all big towns of India and

82

other countries in Asia and Europe, as well as America and Australia. Even the Union Jack at Lahore and parts of India was seen at half mast on the government buildings.

Besides being a great political genius and a courageous leader of the Indian public opinion he was a great educationist as well. I owe a special debt of gratitude to him as I have quoted profusely from his works in the interest of the future system of Indian education that we want to have for the good of all my countrymen and women. In his book, *The Problem of National Education in India,* while criticizing the Britain-Imposed System of Education he makes these comments on the industrial inefficiency in India, "Industrial inefficiency of India is very dangerous. We must devise a system of education in which will fit the future generations of India for the battle of life on modern lines." Here we find him as a great statesman with a vision. He recommends a wide-ranging system of vocational education and says that "every man must find out what he is fitted to do and then secure an opportunity to do it."

On the evils of too early specialization which are ignored by independent India's ministry of education he says, "A very early determination of the occupation is not good for his (pupil's) development intellectually and morally although it may add to his technical efficiency", here he proves himself to be a great educationist, "Consequently all earlier preparations for vocations should be indirect rather than direct."

He further adds, "The first requisite of an efficient system of education is that it enables every citizen to live better and to help others to live better. We must raise the average intellectual standard and the standard of scientific knowledge of our nationals. It is a machine age. It is an age of large scale production and of specialization and complex business, of by-products or "allied industries". Without the wide use of former waste products few large enterprises could now maintain themselves. The by-products are at times the chief source of profits."

He further observes, "Wars are now virtually fought in schools... Universal education of the best modern type is therefore an absolute necessity for the future security of India... Universal popular education must be provided by the state and should be the first charge on state revenues. ...A national system of education must be provided for, enforced, financed and controlled by the State."

A good patriot as he was to the core of his being, he stressed, like Hardayal, on teaching of patriotism in education. In fact all great personalities of the world have cherished great love for their countries and Shri Lajpat Rai was no exception to this rule. Lokmanya Tilak had declared, "*Mother and motherland are greater than heaven.* Let every school going child write this beautiful line several times on his or her notebook by way of exercise in calligraphy. Let every school have this motto hung in some prominent place in the schools for children to read it daily." Swami Vivekananda once said, "Indians are my brothers – Indians are my life, India's Gods and Goddesses are my God, India's society is the cradle of my childhood, the pleasure-garden of my youth, the sacred seclusion of my old age, India's soil is my highest heaven, India's good is my good." Nelson once said, "England, with all thy faults, I love thee." Shakespeare also sang praises of his country thus, "The precious gem set in the silver sea." Similarly India is for every man and woman of India a bright triangular diamond crystal floating on the velvety blue. So Lajpat Rai also says on the teaching of patriotism, we should cherish, "Love of all things Indian: rivers, hills, landscape scenes, animals, cows and bullocks, trees like *pipal*, the great *chinar*, the tall poplar, the sacred *bo* tree, fruits, the kingly mango, the guava, the orange, the banana, the mango stem, the grape, the melon, corns and cereals, pulses and oilseeds, vegetables and roots..." Thus, this great soul's love for India had permeated all things Indian, such was his patriotism.

He further states, "It should be made absolutely clear to every Indian youth that in India there is no such thing as the conflict of races... There is no country on the face of the globe which has a pure race. Desires for political domination and economic exploitation are at the bottom of 'yellow peril[53]' and 'black peril[54]' cries...

"Common country, common political and economic interests, common history and common destiny are to be inculcated through books". Love of our country, cherishing, of course, a respectful regard for other countries should be one of the aims in education. Here and from what follows we see the great statesman, a seer and a great educationist in one.

On the place of physical education in the scheme of education he says: "The two tests of efficiency of a government are (1) low death rate and (2) provision for public education. The health and mental equipment of every unit of the body politic are matters of national concern."

In matters of health and education individual freedom is not recognized. The state concerns itself not just with education and health of its existing citizens, but it goes further and regulates the birth and training of its future members too. From this motive proceed the ever-increasing interests which various governments in the world are showing in the study of eugenics (science of race improvement by judicious mating) in making different kinds of provisions for motherhood including their care and comfort during pregnancy and confinement as also providing from public funds for the care and education of children from birth up to puberty. In a way Lajpat Rai brings the study of the science of eugenics and its place in future marital reforms and family planning and the folly of encouraging/tolerating communal schools in India into the limelight. He also recommends thorough medical examinations of school going children at regular intervals of time.

He further says, "The two things which are of the greatest importance to every human being are health and ability to earn a decent livelihood... We learn too much of Shakespeare, Shelley, Kalidasa and Firdausi etc., but we are not taught how to cultivate an erect posture, how to take care of our bodies, hands, legs, noses, eyes, teeth, ears, (reproductive) organs, muscles and nerves. We know nothing of the hygiene of living, of houses, of food, of dress and of mating. The curriculum of studies neither takes cognizance of these things nor of those which provide recreation and amusement of a healthy and edifying character, no taste for music, no normal health, no attention towards the study of physical education of our school population." In compiling our school textbooks and children's books, we have to take note of these things".

Lajpat Rai has quoted the views of Annie Besant[55] on National Education. She says: "Nothing can more swiftly emasculate national life, nothing can more surely weaken national character than allowing the education of the young to be controlled by foreign influences, to be dominated by foreign ideals. From 1896 onwards I have ventured to urge on the Indian people that the education which was given to their sons was de-nationalizing and de-spiritualizing. Foreign habits, foreign manners, foreign dress, foreign ways all are enforced in a foreign language, within missionary schools a foreign religion to boot, sterilizing the boy's heart and de-spiritualizing his whole nature. Is it any wonder that the national spirit decayed until a vigorous effort was made to capture education by ..."

Coming to the constructive side of the problem Mrs. Besant propounds the question 'what must our national education be?' and then answers it in the following words:

(a) It must be controlled by Indians, shaped by Indians, carried on by Indians. It must hold up Indian ideals of devotion, wisdom and morality and must be permeated by the Indian religious spirit rather than fed on the letter of the creeds. That spirit is spacious, tolerant, all-embracing and recognizes that man goes to God along many roads and that all the prophets came from Him.

(b) National education must live in an atmosphere of proud and glorious patriotism and this atmosphere must be kept sweet, fresh and bracing by the study of Indian literature, Indian history, Indian triumphs in science, in art, in politics, in war, in colonization, in manufactures, in trade, in commerce. The *Arth Shastra* must be studied as well as the *Dharma Shastra*, science and politics as well as religion.

(c) National education must not be separated from the homes of the nation. The ideals, the interests, the principles, the emotions of the one must be those of the other. For the nation is built out of families and the present opposition between the home and the school must cease. The teachers in school and college must work in harmony with the teachers in the home.

(d) National education must meet the national temperament at every point and develop the national character. India is not to become a lesser – nor even a greater – England, but to evolve into a mightier India. British ideals are good for Britain, but it's Indian ideals that are good for India. We do not want echoes nor monotones, we want a choral melody of nations, mirroring the varied qualities of nature and of God. Shall nature show but a single color and trees and flowers and mountains and sky wear but a single hue? Harmonious variety and not monotony is the mark of perfection.

"Away with all apologies for India with all deprecatory explanations of India's ways and customs and traditions. India is herself and needs not to be justified; for verily, God has evolved no greater, no more exquisite nationality than India's among all the broken reflections of His own perfect beauty." She declared emphatically.

Shri Lajpat Rai adds, "There is a general complaint about the multiplicity of subjects in the school curriculum resulting in the impairment of the health of the scholars as well as in making them mere cramming machines. Now, the complaint is well-founded so far as the effects are concerned. An education which impairs the health of the recipient thereof is not worth having. But the fault lies not with the subjects or their number but with the method in which they are taught." This is a very important point as far as I can see. I would add to the number of existing subjects for the broad based education towards improvement in the outlook of our students and to open new avenues of employment to cut down the unemployment and to stimulate human intellect in a variety of fields to make our country self-supporting and self-sufficient as far as possible. But the method of teaching must be greatly improved so that the abundance of subjects instead of being a source of burden on the brains of our students should be a source of recreation and yield a variety of mental food for nourishing their minds. Of course, after acquiring rudimentary knowledge of a rich variety of subjects, there should be full liberty for students to select the subjects they best like. No subject should be forced on them which they do not like. It is the forced subjects, and not their numbers, which they are compelled to take up against their will to pass the examination in the present mechanical and most artificial and inelastic system that destroys the students' health.

"The art of teaching in India takes no cognizance of the individual boy or girl. It is a kind of mechanical process aimed at filling the scholar's mind and body with so many facts and figures. The individual boy or girl is treated as a kind of clay, which the teacher is required to shape, after a given pattern, filling it with so much stuff of a particular stereotyped kind. The prevalent idea seems to be that the boys and girls exist for school teachers and not the latter for the former. The teacher cares more for examinations and discipline than for the mind and the body of his students. The aim before him is to finish so many pages within a given time, and to prove to the examiner, whenever he comes, that the boy remembers what he has been taught." This is the farce played out in the name of education.

"I wonder" goes on Shri Lajpat Rai, "if there is one among a thousand teachers in India who thinks, or who has been told that the real purpose of education is to help the child to become a thinking and acting person... The broad aim of education is to help him to become a thinking man. Life is mostly thinking and acting. Reading and writing are only the means to enable human beings to become better thinkers and actors. The filling of memory and the discipline form very minor parts of the life of a human being. Yet instruction in schools and colleges in India is mostly made up of the latter. Nay, active steps are taken in most schools and colleges to put down thinking and action.

Independence of thought and action is banished and obedience and cramming are rewarded and admired.

"The inspecting officers never fail to record their opinions about the discipline of the school inspected but they never note whether the teaching was directed toward the development of the faculty of thinking. Doing, of course, is not contemplated by the curriculum of studies at all. Indian schools never take notice of the fact that the eye, the hand and the mind are meant for other purposes than that of handling the books, reading the printed letter and committing to memory what is taught..."

That is why we call our schools *Pathshalas* or houses where we do the reading or *Path*. That is to say, they are only reading rooms. So every student has to pass through the same eyehole of the needle and means, and wrong means too, are considered far more important than the ends of education.

He goes on to observe, "Complaints of this kind as to the principles and methods of teaching are quite common even in such advanced countries like Great Britain and the United States of America. The system in operation in India, however, is about fifty years behind that of other countries; and we shall have to make enormous efforts to bring it up to the level of what is already being done in other countries. The task is one of educating the instructors and the educators; of creating public opinion and of enforcing its decisions."

Lala Lajpat Rai further recommends, "reverence for the child". The child should not be molded like clay to a given pattern. It should be given freedom of growth and of judgment. We should produce thought in the child and not belief. The belief will come in due course and of itself. No religious dogmas or doctrines should be taught in schools as they only serve to narrow down the outlook of the child, stop independent development of the mind. Moreover, these are, as yet, beyond the child's comprehension. Tender years are the right time to sow the seeds of truthfulness and good deportment among the young students in order to create sound foundations for further search after truth later on, when their mind is fully developed.

He further writes against "teaching of false history" to our children and quotes Mr. Bertrand Russell[56], an eminent educationalist, as saying, "History in every country is so taught as to magnify that country; children learn to believe that their own country has always been in the right; and almost always victorious, that it has produced almost all the great men and that it is in all respects superior to all other countries. Since these beliefs are flattering they are easily absorbed and hardly ever dislodged from instinct by later knowledge... If the facts about battle of Waterloo[57], for instance, were taught accurately in both countries of England and Germany, national pride would not be fostered to the same extent, neither nation would feel so certain of victory in the event of war and the willingness to fight would be diminished. It is this result which has to be prevented. Every state wishes to promote national pride and is conscious that this cannot be done by unbiased history. The defenseless children are taught by distortions and suppressions and suggestions. The false ideas as to the history of the world which are taught in the various countries are of a kind which encourages strife and serves to keep alive a bigoted nationalism."

In this way a clear lead is provided to the country in the teaching of the Indian History that still remains to be written.

I have made a humble attempt in this direction after a lot of research work. I have yet seen no truthful and complete history of the Indian people beginning with the true *Vedic* Age up to the present times, i.e., 1961.

You can love your country to the full without, of course, sacrificing truth and even with the full knowledge of her (India's) frailties and shortcomings, as you love your mother knowing fully well that she is not an image of perfection in every way. Our nationalism should have its roots in the equality, oneness and sanctity of all life. It should transcend our country's borders and cover the entire planet as one connected piece. It should go further and reach the most distant limits of the infinite expanse and we should pray in love for the good of all that lives in this wide universe. Indian children are to be taught to worship the memory of their great patriots like Gandhi, Jawaharlal Nehru and Lakshmi Bai the Rani of Jhansi, Ramakrishna, Buddha, Mahavir Swami, Nanak, Chaitanya, Guru Gobind, Rana Pratap, Shivaji, Prithvi Raj, Chhattrasal, Banda Vairagi, Durga Dass Rathor, Padmani, Sita, Anusuya, Savitri, Lakshmi Pandit, Sarojini, Mira, Abdul Ghaffar Khan, Dayananda, Shradhananda, Vivekananda, Ram Tirath, Ramakrishna Paramhansa, Tilak, Lajpat Rai, Dadabhai Naoroji, Ravi Varma and B.K. Mitra (painters), C.R. Das, Moti Lal Nehru, Rabindra Nath Tagore, Subhash Chandra Bose, Jagdish Chandra Bose, Valmiki, Vyas, Patanjali, Kalidasa, Tulsi Das, Surdas, Kapil[58], Kanad[59], Gautam, Jaimini, Dadhichi, Prahlad, Dhruv, Puran, Bharat, Shankaracharya, Shibi, Ranti Dev, Bhishampitamah, Vidur, Samudragupta, Ashoka, Harashvardhan, Chandragupta, Vikramaditya, Harish Chandra, Janak and innumerable other great men and women of India from varied walks of life. They have to show a similar respectful regard for Leo Tolstoy of Russia, Confucius and Sun Yat-Sen of China, Jesus Christ of Palestine, Saint Thoreau of the U.S.A., Joan of Arc of France, Nelson of England, Mazzini and Garibaldi of Italy and Leonidas of Greece, Alfred Bernhard Nobel of Sweden, Kemal Ataturk of Turkey and Reza Shah Pehalvi of Persia. And these are only a few of the great personalities who belong to all nations alike.

However, that education is much more than an academic phenomenon becomes clear from the fact that the British Raj authorities had used it as a political tool for consolidating their power in the subcontinent. It also provides a platform for interaction that can be employed either to get rid of prejudices and stereotypes or to reinforce mutual contempt – depending upon the extant official policy. Needless to say, such a role for education is undesirable.

Shri P.M. Mehta in his speech at Bombay Graduate Association on April 4, 1893, said, "The process by which a B.A. B.T (qualifications for trained graduate teachers) contributes his share of work towards the consolidation of British authority in India, the whole scheme was as clear as daylight to the founders of the educational system. The educational system brings Indians into close contact with Englishmen and thus encourages mutual regard and esteem. It weakens the feeling of aversion and contempt with which all conquered nations at first regard their foreign rulers who are different from them in religion, manners and language. It promotes social intercourse between the rulers and the ruled and softens racial animosities. It cuts at the root of the instinctive repugnance born of patriotism with which all races regard their conquerors in the period immediately following the conquest when the sores are not healed and bitter memories separate the two communities like a river of blood. Thus the educational system supplies a point of contact between the rulers and the ruled. The pupil cannot divest himself of all respect for his teacher. The violence of force, racial hatred and prejudice on the part of the ruled is really tempered and allayed by the relations that subsist between the teacher and the taught. The gift of knowledge tends to blunt the edge of resentment felt at the loss of national dignity and self respect..."

Shri Rash Behari Ghosh[60] and Lokmanya Bal Gangadhar Tilak had similar pronouncements on national education. But as these great thinkers and leaders of public opinion were in the thick of the political fight for freedom, they were kept too busy by the resourceful foreign government and hence they could not pay much attention to educational reforms.

In his speeches and writings, and under the heading, *Education on National Lines*, Swami Vivekananda says, "The present education is not man-making education. It is merely and entirely a negative education... The child is taken to school and the first thing he learns there is that his father was a fool, the second his grandfather was a crazy lunatic, the third that all his teachers were hypocrites, the fourth that all the sacred books were lies! By the time he is sixteen he is a mass of negation, lifeless and boneless..."

Beyond the hopeless school textbooks the Indian youth was further tried to be fed on mischievous literature created in other countries and stones were thrown at India from other peoples' housetops to mislead world public opinion and to degrade India in the eyes of the world. A book, *Mother India,* was got written by British diplomats through Miss Mayo[61], an

American national, or perhaps it was ascribed to her to throw cold water on India's political aspirations and to create bad blood between India and the United States of America; for there were some good people in that freedom loving country who honestly sympathized with India in her struggle for political independence as they had themselves passed through similar ordeal. The British diplomats thought, perhaps, that the scheme would serve their purpose. It would deceive the world who would think that in the opinion of the United States of America also India was not fit for self-government and nobody would doubt the honest intentions of Britain about India. Secondly, some self-respecting, patriotic Indians might be tempted to write, by way of reply/rejoinder, something against the United States of America, as some actually did, which would lead to deterioration of relationship between the two countries. India would thus lose U.S.A's. active sympathy and goodwill in her struggle for independence. Thirdly, the book would create an atmosphere of ill will in India against the United States of America – the rising power that was considered by Britain as its rival in the field of trade and colonial possessions; the chances of America's trade with India would be considerably reduced and the possibilities of her political ambitions in India, if any, according to the British, would be greatly minimized.

Mahatma Gandhi's views on education

In the words of Gandhiji this (Britain-Imposed) education is "defective in three most important matters", viz.:
1.   It is based on foreign culture to the almost entire exclusion of the indigenous culture. "Almost from the commencement the textbooks deal not with things the boys and girls have always to deal with in their homes but things to which they are perfect strangers. It is not through the textbooks that a lad learns what is right and what is wrong in the home life. He is never taught to have any pride in his surroundings. The higher he goes the farther he is removed from his home, so that at the end of his education he becomes estranged from his surroundings. He feels

no poetry about the home life. The village scenes are all a sealed book to him. His own civilization is presented to him as imbecile, barbarous, superstitious and useless for all practical purposes. His education is calculated to wean him away from his traditional culture. And if the mass of educated youth is not entirely denationalized it is because the ancient culture is too deeply embedded in them to be altogether uprooted even by an education adverse to its growth. If I had my way I would certainly destroy the majority of the present textbooks and cause to be written textbooks which have a bearing on, and correspondence with, the home life so that a boy may react upon his immediate surroundings."

2. It ignores the culture of the heart and the hand and confines itself to the head.

3. Real education is impossible through foreign medium. The foreign medium was regarded by Gandhiji as the greatest tragedy of the modern system. "The foreign medium" says Mahatma Gandhi, "has caused brain-fag, put an undue strain upon the nerves of our children, made them crammers and imitators unfitted for original work and thought, and disabled them from filtrating their learning to the family or the masses. The foreign medium has made our children practically foreigners in their own land."

Gandhiji's Wardha Scheme of Education[62]

Gandhiji's Wardha scheme of education laid emphasis on handwork. 'Earning while learning' should be the aim. Education in a poor country like India, thought Gandhiji, must be economically self-sufficient. Since India cannot find two thousand million rupees as annual expenses for the education of all school-going children, this was the considered solution for the financial difficulties. Education in American universities is closely related to the industry and other needs of the country, he points out. Similarly, education in India too ought to be relevant to its current needs and future aspirations.

This system of education, however, has created a gulf between the educated few and the illiterate many. This learning (by one individual student) does not infiltrate even to the family, much less to the masses. It gives light only to scholars while keeping the masses in the dark.

Shri Rabindra Nath Tagore also expressed a similar idea when he said, "Foreign system of education is like a lamp in the railway compartment. The room is brilliantly lit, but thousands of miles traversed by the train remain shrouded in the darkness as before."

Views of the First Five Year Planning Board

"Defects of the existing system: Enormous wastage of educational effort, particularly at the earliest stages (pupils discontinuing within the first three years), has not succeeded in training the intellect, developing practical efficiency, and inculcating moral and social values. The majority of students fail to develop the necessary spirit of enquiry, balanced judgment, habit of application and capacity for striking out new paths which are the attributes of a sound system of educational training. At the same time, the qualities which make for moral development and sound character are neglected. (The end result of the present system is) a noticeable growth of indiscipline among students, excessively low value in employment market, not even giving efficient service in government departments for which they were originally designed; and poor adaptability to new surroundings or avenues of work.

"Objectives:- Immediate objective: Adaptability to the requirements of national planning; development of the individual. It has to train the senses, develop the intellect, humanize the emotions and equip the individual for efficient living for the growth of his personality and efficient service of the social order which is the object of the national planning to evolve.

"Lack of coordination that exists between the home, the school and the life outside has to be removed and a close integration secured between the process of education and the social and economic life of the country."

Further, there is no gradation in educational development in India through this system. In fact the primary standard is maintained throughout. The same amount of instruction is going on in different mediums at different levels: what is taught in vernaculars in the lower standards is repeated in English in the higher standards, or in different arrangements – with minor changes in details here and there. There are the same uniform, stereotyped and inelastic curricula for different kinds of intellect entailing great waste of time and energy and dulling of the students' wits. Hundreds of spheres of intellectual development are not even touched, let alone explored, because both the basis (the medium of instruction) and the aims of educational practice (producing clerical labor) are wrong.

Educational process must cease to be merely bookish and mechanical as it is seen to be today. Books should be treated as aids to the acquiring of knowledge; these should not turn into oppressive prisons wherein a child's originality, imagination, observation and independent thinking are locked up and crushed under heavy schoolbags. The curriculum should not become a constant reminder of the date of examination and thus turning it into a doomsday of sorts for the school going child. In fact the fear factor, vis-à-vis exams, is a direct result of the extant system.

This Britain-Imposed System of education has provided us with, of course in rare cases, palatial school buildings that have given a false sense of satisfaction, lulling us to sleep vis-à-vis our quest for genuine education. Imposing school buildings also served as tools for propaganda in the colonial times that our educational needs had been well attended to by the British Government. With great buildings, however, they gave us poor equipment and library and poorer staff and the poorest quality of curricula. The result was, therefore, disappointing. Our present B.As and M.As from this system are, truly speaking, mostly Bachelors of Arrogance and Masters of Arrogance and B.SCs and M.SCs are Bachelors and Masters of Scholastic-

Confusion respectively. If some of them are not like this, it is not because of the system, but despite the system; moreover other influence leave their effect too, such as religious and social movements, heredity, environments, *satvik* temper of the individuals or some special effort on the part of those individuals to improve themselves on their own. We could not expect better results from education at the hands of a foreign power that had decided to rule over us for all time.

V. Some recent trends in education in India

Two important publications are worthy of attention for the present, viz., (1) Mahatma Gandhi's Wardha Scheme of Primary Education; and (2) its confusing and mischievous corollary, the Sargent proposals[63], otherwise known as Post War Educational Development in India: Report by the Central Advisory Board of Education January 1944.

Gandhiji's Wardha scheme of education laid emphasis on handwork. Moreover, it advocates earning while learning as the primary aim. Education in a poor country like India, thought Gandhiji, must be economically self-sufficient. Since India cannot generate annual funding to the tune of two thousand million rupees for providing education to all school going children, this solution was mooted while keeping the financial difficulties in view[64].

According to him the extant system of education has created a gulf between the educated few and the illiterate many. This learning does not infiltrate even to the family, much less to the masses. Consequently, it provides light only to scholars but fails to illuminate the path of the masses.

I am sorry I have not been able to secure a copy of Gandhiji's Scheme in original as I am in a foreign country. I have, therefore, tried to make the best use of some other books available here by eminent writers that throw some light on the said scheme.

Mahatma Gandhi, during the British regime, had recommended to the nation the boycott of all educational institutions in the country as an integral part of his noncooperation movement. The boycott movement against educational institutions gained some momentum for a while but failed because, I think, it was not possible for the country to do sufficient construction work in the educational field side by side with the destructive one, especially when the country was in a state of nonviolent war with the all-resourceful and well-established foreign government. In spite of the fact that Mahatma Gandhi, the commander-in-chief of India's nonviolent forces, was very busy organizing different fronts of the battlefield he seized some moments to offer something to the nation by way of constructive work in the educational field and the result was, I think, the Wardha Scheme of Primary Education. So it was all, in my opinion, an ad hoc or emergency measure and cannot therefore be taken as a fully thrashed-out plan or perfectly thought out or accurate concept of education system that could meet the entire and complex needs of India. Moreover, primary education is not the only problem the nation has to tackle.

The four fundamental principles of this scheme according to Shri S.N. Mukerji in his book *Education in India in the XX Century* were: "(1) Free and compulsory education for seven years on a nationwide scale; (2) Mother tongue as medium of instruction; (3) The instruction must centre round some form of manual work and all other abilities to be developed, or training to be given, should be – as far as possible – integrally related to the central handicraft chosen with due regard to the environment of the child; and (4) The system of education should be so devised that it might gradually cover the remuneration of teachers."

Shrimati Amrit Kaur, Health Minister, in a book *Gandhiji as an Educationist* authored by Shri Vishvanath Sahai Mathur, says about Gandhiji: "He held that book-knowledge, however useful and necessary, could never take the place of knowledge gained by 'doing'. In other words his theory of education lay in bringing out the best in the child and in the adult, the best in them, by stimulating their creative impulses. Above all he laid the greatest stress on the moral and spiritual values of life without which all else is worthless."

"The basic principle of the Gandhi Scheme", says Shri Vishwanath Sahai Mathur, "is 'creative activity', an all-round harmonious development of the students' personality... a spiritual refashioning of the whole personality of the pupil through activity and craft.

"The society may place before a child a number of channels and opportunities for asking for and acquiring knowledge. A child must be free to pick and choose.

"According to the scheme a school is to have opportunities for learning five or six arts and crafts and these arts and crafts should be related to the satisfaction of the basic material needs of all humanity, such as food, clothing, housing, health and recreation. The children who go into school are to be given the freedom to flirt with all the available opportunities presented by the school, ask for as much information as they feel like about them, try to learn various processes and slowly indicate their preferences and finally make their choice of one or two or more arts and crafts. Thus, Gandhiji reached his conception of teaching through arts and crafts, work and play, voluntary activity and self-chosen enquiry.

"The role that a teacher can play in such a school is to be a lamp-post, a sign board, a reference book, a dictionary, a dissolvent, a compound processor... Certainly a woman finds it easier to become such a teacher than a man. That is why a child generally prefers to learn more from a mother than from father.

"The only criterion for a suitable craft was that it should be rich in educational possibilities, correlated with life easily, and had the local conditions in its favor.

"Basic education based on the psychological principles of play and activity was made joyous and creative by Gandhiji. There is no slavery or unwilling labor in it. The process of activity as opposed to the deadweight of information from books unrelated to life brings a wave of joy to the child's mind and body."

Shri Vishvanath Sahai Mathur further expresses the views of Mahatma Gandhi on national education as saying: "National education, to be truly national, must reflect the national condition for the time being... How do children fare in a besieged place? Do they not, according to their capacity, take part in repelling the attack of the besiegers and suit themselves to the changing circumstances? Is not that their true education? Is not education the art of drawing out full manhood of the children under training? The greatest drawback of the present system of education is that it does not bear the stamp of reality that the children do not react to the varying needs of the country. True education must correspond to the surrounding circumstances or it is not a healthy growth..." Mr. Mathur adds, "According to him (Gandhiji) the object of basic education was the physical, intellectual and moral development of children through the medium of a handicraft..."

Says Gandhiji, "In my opinion intelligent labor is, for the time being, the only primary and adult education in this land of starving millions... Literary education should follow the education of the hand – the one gift that visibly distinguishes man from beast. It is a superstition to think that the fullest development of man is impossible without knowledge of the art of reading and writing. That knowledge undoubtedly adds grace to life, but it is in no way indispensable for man's moral, physical or material growth. Manual work will have to be the very centre of the whole thing... The manual training will not consist in producing articles for a school museum or toys which have no value. It should produce marketable articles. The children will not do this as children used to do under the whip in the early days of the factories. They will do it because it entertains them and stimulates their intellect... My plan to impart primary education through the medium of village handicrafts like spinning and carding etc is thus conceived as the spearhead of a silent social revolution fraught with the most far-reaching consequences. It will provide a healthy and moral basis of relationship between the city and the village and thus go a long way towards eradicating some of the worst evils of the present social insecurity and poisoned relationship between the classes... Man is neither mere intellect, nor the gross animal body, nor the heart or soul alone. A proper and harmonious combination of all the three is required for the making of the whole man and constitutes the true economics of education."

"In other countries", says Shri Mathur, "Learning through Activity, the Loveback system, the Project Method, exist of similar pattern as Gandhi's method, the Wardha Scheme.

"All localities should be studied for basic crafts suited to local conditions. This craft becomes the medium of instruction and through it other subjects are taught. So far as possible the whole of the curriculum is harmonized with this general conception. Rousseau, Froebel, Montessori, and Margaret Macmillan have contributed towards the growth of this idea of education through activity, though its use varies from school to school in Europe and America. Some schools are more progressive than others. That is to say, they give more of the Robinson Crusoe type of education and less of the copybook and printed type, more of the three H's (head, hand and heart) and less of the three R's. Mahatma Gandhi studied this system and adapted it to Indian conditions. According to him its fundamentals are: 'You practice what you learn – it is education for life and for life in India – pupils are to be self-sustaining in food, clothing, cooking, sanitation and community service – while they study they are to be self-sustaining."

Shri Mathur further avers, "According to Gandhiji literacy in itself is no education. Literacy merely signifies more information on various methods through reading and writing and capacity to follow logical or pseudo-logical controversy. It is, according to him, not even knowledge or even the medium of knowledge. How very true he was when he declared that literacy may be regarded as only a symbolical representation both of knowledge and of accomplished ignorance. True education to him was 'An all round drawing out of the best in child and man – body, mind and spirit. Literacy, he went on, is not the end of education, nor even the beginning of it. It is only one of the means whereby men and women can be educated...

"The question as to how the basic scheme of education would fit into the secondary system was tackled by Gandhiji: 'The task was', he said, 'to devise a diversified system of institutions to provide whole-time education for various aptitude types on the basis of education through work, keeping in view the needs of national life. This is a generously conceived, complete system of life regarding education suiting the different aptitudes, abilities and needs of adolescents but not ignoring the requirements of national life. The post-Basic syllabuses have therefore to be formulated on a wide basis satisfying the requirements of university, technical and professional education as also our contacts with the world. Therefore, the question of banishment of world languages, of modern sciences and technical knowledge does not arise. If narrower syllabuses have been framed, they will not stand the test of time. Gandhiji could complete the details of secondary education. He never attempted to define in detail the system of national education."

Comments of Shri K.G. Saiyidain on Wardha Scheme, in his book *Problems of Educational Reconstruction*: "Gandhi's Scheme of Primary Education that it should centre not around books but around rural crafts closely related to the life and activities of the village... In rural schools there should be framing of syllabus in social studies, and General Science should be closely related to real problems of rural life... This is not new educational doctrine... More recently, through educational movements like the Project Method and the Activity School, this doctrine has been given a place of honor in schools of Europe and America and Soviet Russia. We should strike a right balance between the practical and the cultural objectives."

The how and why of Sir John Sargent's proposals

Mr. Macaulay's proposals (1835) in the British Parliament, determining Indian Educational Policy, which had been forced down India's throat for about a century, were very unpopular and the movement under the leadership of

Mahatma Gandhi was gathering momentum. However, it hardly disturbed the British bureaucracy's sangfroid in India. With a view to circumvent the movement, they created in 1935 a bogus body of 'yes' men, which was called the Central Advisory Board of Education. It functioned under Sargent, the then Educational Advisor to the Viceroy. It produced a report called "Post War Educational Development in India or Report by the Central Advisory Board of Education" in January 1944. This Report was written not to make an honest and serious effort to build up the system of education on new lines based on the instinct of the people or fitting the present and future needs of the country but just to prepare a hotchpotch of an educational puzzle to silence the Agitator and waylay the Reformer. At first the Central Advisory Board set up two committees one after the other under the chairmanship of B.G. Kher, the former Premier and Minister of Education of Bombay Presidency for considering the Wardha Scheme.

Proposals of the First Kher Committee

The first committee submitted its report in June 1938. The main recommendations were: "(1) The scheme of Basic education should first be introduced in rural areas; (2) The age of compulsion should be six to fourteen years but children can be admitted to the Basic School at the age of five; (3) Diversion of students from the 'basic' school to other kinds of schools should be allowed after the fifth class or at about the age of eleven plus (Is it in keeping with modern educational theory and practice? It smacks of the 3 R's and the eighteenth century model of teaching!); (4) Certain elements of cultural subjects which cannot be correlated to the basic craft must be taught independently; (5) No teacher should receive less than Rs. 20/- per month (Would that have attracted, even in 1938, good educated people to this profession? Even a coolie on an Indian Railway Station in 1938 was earning more per month); (6) English should not be introduced as an optional subject in 'basic' schools; and (7) No external examination need be held at the end of the 'basic' school course, a leaving certificate based on internal examination should be given. Promotion from class to class will be determined by the school, though the results of the internal examination should be subject to supervisor's inspection."

Proposals of the Second Kher Committee

The Second Kher Committee published its report in 1940. The main recommendations were: (1) Basic education should comprise a course of eight years from 6 to 14 years of age; and that this course, while preserving its essential unity, should consist of two stages – the first stage, the 'junior' stage, covering a period of 5 years and the second or 'senior' stage, three years; (2) The transfer of children from the Basic School to other forms of post-primary education should be allowed at the conclusion of the 'junior' basic stage (Was the proposal found sound educationally even when it came for reconsideration in the second committee? Did any advanced country of the world allow this parting of the ways so early in the life of the child even in 1940?); (3) Suitable course should be framed for girls attending 'senior basic' schools which should include such subjects as cookery, laundry work, needlework, home crafts, the care of children and first aid, the remainder of instruction to be correlated to the course of domestic science in accordance with the general principles of the basic education scheme; and (4) The various types of post-primary schools (other than the 'senior basic' school) to which suitable children may be transferred at the end of the 'junior basic' stage should provide a variety of course options extending over a period of at least five years after the age of eleven (But will this give us hundreds of thousands of women teachers and lady-doctors and midwives wanted for the present and the future needs of the country? How would you determine the 'suitability' of a child at the age of eleven for a particular industry or occupation? The examination marks constitute too fragile a reed to lean upon. More often than not they prove unreliable. The industrial or commercial bias could be given in the senior basic classes themselves without interfering with the all round cultural development of the child. Similarly it would be difficult to find out "a sure measuring rod", as Shri Mukerji has put it, to measure the 'ability' of students for the High School and the University).

The introductory remarks of the Report

But how far the reports of these two committees and more than thirty other reports of other committees appointed by the Central Advisory Board have helped Sir John Sargent to prepare his draft proposals for a well planned system of education for India is not clear. The Introduction to the report *Post-War Educational Development in India* showing the scope of his work for the educational uplift of India makes for interesting reading. In the beginning of the introduction he talks of the "British System of Education" but in the case of India he is content with the "System of Public Instructions".

He further says: "It is for India to decide whether the time has arrived when a national system of education is a paramount necessity." This shows that the author, perhaps, still believed that the time for a national system of education had not yet arrived for India, but he would like to invite opinions of others on the same. Perhaps some of the chosen few around him might say that the time was not yet ripe for it and the proposal might be relegated to the cold storage, or someone among them might say that there was, of course, some necessity for further development of the old order (not full-fledged new system of education suitable to India's needs) but even that necessity was not of the 'paramount' variety.

He further goes on to say, "Since the primary object of this report is to place a practicable plan of post-war development before the Reconstruction Committee of the Viceroy's Executive Council, which will hardly have the time or the desire to concern itself with matters of educational method or technique, only such reference will be made to the contents of these reports (of the committees set up by CAB) as may be necessary to elucidate the general principles upon which the Board's present recommendations are based."

This Report's contents clearly indicated that the Board was not going to take up the comprehensive question of a new system of education to replace the previous one; the country sorely needed an educational structure and policy which should suit India's national instinct, aims and aspirations. The Report was only a 'development' or extension of the same nonsensical and soulless education with which India had all along been burdened. The said Report was written in 1944 during the British rule. How could the ex-Advisor on Educational matters to the then Viceroy be expected to condemn that old wretched system? So this new effort by the same person in his new capacity as Educational Advisor to the Government of a free and sovereign India meant only to try to satisfy the country by carrying out some small cosmetic patchworks in the old scheme; like its emphasis on increasing some small percentage of literacy in the country and that too at a heavy cost to the country through much wastage of money in wrong channels, which in forty long years failed to solve the real problems bedeviling the vital areas of education. Moreover, it appears that all the reports of the different committees have been considerably watered down as could be seen in his final Report which is further hedged by the use of such epithets and phrases as 'practicable', 'minimum', 'necessary', 'within the general lines laid down' etc – which not only limited the scope of any implementation of sound education policy but were misleading per se. Please note the bureaucratic way of handling this inglorious effort in 1944 which was to be put before the Reconstruction Committee of the Viceroy's Executive Council "which would not have the time or even the desire to concern itself with matters of educational method and technique"! What was the use of such a Viceroy or his Executive Council to this country if he or they had 'no time or even a desire' to show any concern for such an important problem like education of this country? Could the Education Minister of

Britain have the audacity to use such words and show lack of interest for the educational needs of his country? Had he done so, he would have been dismissed on grounds of neglect of duty or even insanity. It is a thousand pities that this Report, which was written by the same reactionary, Mr. Sargent, during the British regime, and which should have been condemned and discarded after the country's freedom, has been made the basis of educational development of the same Britain Imposed System for education in India and under his leadership! The money that was being spent by way of salary to such an officer or on the development of the ruins of a rotten unsanitary structure like the Britain Imposed Model of Education proved to be a sheer waste. The recommendations, in fact, constituted an insult to the intelligence of educated India and have since been a source of mischief, giving a wrong lead to the country especially at a time of reorientation in the educational sphere, as would appear from further instances quoted below.

Sir John Sargent avers, "…. While the Board have aimed at a Standard comparable with those already attained in Great Britain and other western countries before the war, they have been careful not to adopt western ideas or to copy western methods, without being fully satisfied that they are those best suited to India. They also realize that conditions in different parts of India vary greatly and that, consequently, their aim should be to indicate the main lines which development should follow rather than to prescribe any information or detailed plan. It will be for the responsible educational authorities to devise for themselves, within the general lines laid down, the type of education most appropriate to their particular areas, and with this object in view, to give the fullest encouragement to every form of potentially useful experiment."

He has thus sown seeds of disunity and of disintegration in the nascent Republic of India and has made confusion worse confounded. To catch up public imagination and to create public enthusiasm and faith in his leadership he talks of the Board's generous aims of attaining to British standards of education and those of other western countries for the sake of India's

107

educational advancement, but in the same breath he beats a skilful retreat and rejects western ideas and methods as, according to him, they do not suit India and thus leaves his audience gasping and nonplussed. India's educational needs are different in different parts of the country according to Mr. Sargent so no 'uniform' plan of education will suit India, he says. Therefore the different parts of the country should only make 'experiments' in education for the present and see whose experiments are useful! After a study of this report I am sometimes inclined to feel that the process of disrupting India, started by the foreign power about the time of its departure from the country's shores, is still being scrupulously followed by its lingering shadows even after its formal exit.

Mr. Sargent at one place has even talked of the impossibility of India's having any really national system of education at all and in the support of the existing order (the Britain imposed system) he says: "It is certainly not the Board's desire either to exaggerate existing defects or overlook what has been achieved in the face of grave difficulties at certain times and places, but in their considered opinion it is inconceivable that within a reasonable period a really national system could be developed or evolved from what now exists or by the methods hitherto followed."

Then the whole thing boils down to this: that the existing defects of the Britain Imposed System are only to persist ad infinitum and there is no possibility for our country to have any national system of education within a 'reasonable period' of time. At other places he is careful to use the word 'national' before the word education, perhaps, just to cheer us up in our disappointment conveyed to us in the last paragraph. Or, perhaps, he wanted to give an impression of possessing a national perspective on the implementation of the education policy. By merely placing the word 'national' before any system of education you cannot make it national. It must be thoroughly drenched in national culture and national history and linked with national, social and political aspirations and life, and – in the case of India – should have a spiritual aim in the final analysis before it can be called Indian national system of education. In other words the Indian education superstructure must possess an Indian soul.

The proposals of Mr. Sargent have, however, put before us the same old soul-killing, purely materialistic model, the same old wine – that too poorly fermented and decocted – in a new bottle. These proposals moot a system sans cultural foundations without a national medium of education; it is my belief that without the two (Indian culture and history) all education is a farce. It would be just like the play of Hamlet with Hamlet's part left out, a corpse without soul, a wearisome journey without destination. It will be reactionary in design, materialistic in outlook, and an anachronism in makeup. Without cultural basis Indian education would be a poor imitation, a building without foundation, at the mercy of winds, showers and earthquakes and it would produce characterless, soulless pygmies rather than intellectual moral and physical giants. Blind imitation of some of the syllabi of the West (and that too with all their beauties left out as it is done at present in India) would give India only poor education or *Gyana* which would only lead her, like the West, to imperialism, colonialism, atheism, racialism, heartless capitalism, violent communism, triggering off strikes and lockouts, sustaining the constant struggle between labor and capital, class war and international strife. India, according to her cultural demands, requires a different type of education. She wants education or *Gyana* which is full of penance, which has been purified by penance and which alone could lead her to her proper destiny, i.e. peace within the country and friendship with all countries of the world and to her proper place in the comity of nations. So our ideals, our traditions, our social, political, cultural and economic life, our history, our great principles of morality, our fine arts, our literature and our science and technology should fully shine from our system of education; and all this is impossible without reinforcing the essentially secular character of the Indian State.

Sir Sargent appears to be proud of his achievement (of his working of Britain Imposed System) "in the face of grave difficulties at certain times and places." He may be thinking, perhaps, of certain wars which were fought by Britain, of course at the cost of India's resources and winning more lands for the British Empire; or he may be thinking of communal troubles which were only a creation of British policy in India. Besides, 80 crores of rupees were spent annually out of the revenue of a poor country like India on military alone while the nation-building departments starved, and the percentage of literacy 'achieved' during 350 years of British rule was only 8.3% of population including a large percentage of people whose education did not go beyond scribbling their own names!

He further adds to the confusion by saying in his 'Introduction' whether education "might be limited to all the children in some places or some of the children everywhere or some of the children in some places only. Even if such a differentiation could be regarded as compatible with the claim of social justice it is difficult to see how the selection involved could be fairly made. If there is anything like equality of opportunity it is impossible to justify providing facilities for some of the nation's children and not for others." (It is the same old story of distribution of the cake between two cats by the monkey). He goes on, "In the first place, therefore, a national system can hardly be other than universal. Secondly, it must also be compulsory if the grave wastage which exists today under a voluntary system is not to be perpetuated and even aggravated. And, thirdly, if education is to be universal and compulsory, equity requires that it should be free; and commonsense demands that it should last long enough to secure its fundamental objective." So he has used all his ingenuity to confuse the issue as much as possible and has set different parts of India by the ears.

Thus, in his apparent effort to solve one problem of education for India in this paragraph Mr. Sargent has created so many other problems to satisfy his high ideals of "social justice", "equality of opportunity", "equality" and "common sense" and his great longing to see "universal", "free", "compulsory" and full education in India. He has made alert all different parts of the country to see that none of them is left behind, or passed on for the time being, in the race when selection of areas for educational institutions takes place. He has also previously given them the liberty of proposing their own models of education; their 'experiments', probably built on their provincial vernaculars, which disruptive forces are busy in strengthening in the different states to complete at some future date the political dismemberment of the country. He has picked up some of the popular catch-phrases and ideals of our great leaders and exploited them to cause a split and confusion in our ranks. Thus India, which has already been exploded politically, socially and economically at the time of Britain's exit, stands also educationally exploded after the said exit. He has also tried to prove in several ways that India is unable to move forward and have an educational system of her own, of reasonably good standard. Has India decided to accept the old rotten ruts for all time under the leadership of Sir Sargent?

If India, after doing away with the foreign yoke, wants to seek guidance from the same people who have been responsible for keeping her down in education and industry for such a considerable period, who have been maintaining one type of educational system for Britain and quite a different one for India – who have been and are still explaining away the difference between the said two systems due to the different needs and methods of the two countries, and who openly say that there is no possibility for India to have a national system of education of her own choice for a long time to come – then God help India! Sir John Sargent, till the midnight of 15th August 1947, was a cog in the machinery of the alien government, running her educational policy which has thoroughly poisoned our educational system and ethos, as well as our social and political life, with communalism and provincialism; and after India's independence, the same gentleman had the audacity to bless that system for all times to come! Did he change overnight all his previous convictions and principles of education which he followed during the British regime and became a convert now to new ideals of "social justice", "equity", "equality of opportunity" and "commonsense" and so on? Had India not a single educationist of some worth and vision to whom the educational destiny of India could be safely entrusted? Could Sir Sargent be able to build up the new great edifice of Indian education without understanding the culture and social life of the country, and to which he is a complete stranger? Could he be in a position to give a lead to this great country in the educational sphere without being thoroughly conversant with her national language, her national literature and her national ethos? If, in spite of all these serious shortcomings, India has accepted his leadership, then God help India!

Although Britain, during her long rule of 150 years in India, never ever gave us even for a day the British system of education which works in Britain Sargent has been kind enough in his Introduction to the Report to advise us to shape our educational system after that great model (in God's good time, of course) after making all sorts of regional experimentation in education! But Mr. Sargent must know that there are other countries in the world which are ahead of Britain in matters education and we need not intend to make India a cheap copy of Britain in these matters. We have got enough light and commonsense in us to know what is best for our country. In education Britain is behind several countries for the simple reason that her mind has been busy so far in founding and managing her vast colonial empire and in organizing her trade, commerce and markets and thus has had comparatively less time to think of education related matters.

School buildings, Mr. Sargent then tells us, are of primary importance. This is a piece of his precious lead! Poor India has been building-mad all these long years of British rule. She had too many palatial school buildings, with poor equipment and still poorer and starving staff during the British regime. She had a splendid educational body without soul! We can afford to postpone our building program for some time without crippling the vital parts of our educational system, that is to say, we dare not neglect equipment and the proper training and emoluments of our teachers. Let our students have education under trees or in temporary but well-ventilated hutments made of bamboo and grass, decorated with flowers, just to provide protection from sun and rain. We should have only brickworks in the initial stages to house the science gallery, the library, the school museum and a gymnasium as part of a well-planned school building program. The rest of the school building could be completed later on when funds allowed it. But the acquisition of equipment of right quality and quantity must not be delayed nor the training of teachers and their proper emoluments. We must equip our schools with magic lantern[65], cine-projector, radio and television sets as soon as possible. In this way we will not only make the study of subjects like history, geography, hygiene, Hindi etc in the junior basic classes very interesting for our school children but also we will be able to reduce the number of teachers required for the present, in the initial stages, at least to one half as we can easily have a strength of fifty students, instead of the proposed twenty five or thirty for the different stages, in all junior basic classes. We could also cut down to a very large extent the number of books required for school children in different vernaculars in all stages.

Mr. Sargent again is seen anxious to satisfy all communal and caste related requirements in education and gives his support to all communal schools vide paragraph 7, page 4, of the Report. One has failed to understand the necessity for introducing caste and community based stratification into our national education system. This Report is full of mischief as it attempts to create and perpetuate the differences. The same old scales of justice between two cats are in evidence throughout the Introduction. Has Mr. Sargent seen separate educational arrangements in Britain for the education of the English, the Scotch, the Welsh and the North Irish children, the Protestant children and the Catholic children, the Puritan children and the Presbyterian children? Has Britain ever been free from social stratifications that are similar to our caste and community based structure? Who were Jutes[66], Angels[67], Saxons, Danes and Normans[68]? Are capitalistic classes the same as labor classes? What is the meaning of strikes and lock-outs, then, which we come across so often in the British Press? Does a member of the House of Lords like to move about on footings of equality with a factory worker? India has only one class now and that is Indian first and last; and needs no 'impartial' foreign judge to decide things among them. India is seriously thinking of putting to an end all her communal schools and converting them into State schools and thus pull down the hiding places of the demons of communalism and religious fanaticism that have been rampant during the era of foreign domination.

Further, in his proposals, Mr. Sargent puts forward the idea of 'dogmatic religious education' in State schools – thus increasing the possibility of the spread of communal poison – which had ruined all communal schools during the British rule – to all state schools also. Has Mr. Sargent, as an educationist, witnessed arrangements for the teaching of all different types of 'dogmatic religious instruction' in all schools of Britain or elsewhere in Europe or America? Does he know, as an educationist again, and while drawing a generous salary from the Indian State coffers, that morality and not any particular kind of religious dogma is the religion of the schools in France, which is just in the close neighborhood of Britain? By starting a talk on dogmatic religious education in schools he tries to set the ball rolling for further communal mischief and fixes a special committee for the purpose so that if anybody puts the finger on this mischief, the blame may lie at the door of the special committee.

Mr. Sargent avoids discussing, as an educationist, the usefulness or otherwise of too many examinations but jumps to the conclusion at once – without even consulting the Central Advisory Board – that these examinations are absolutely necessary as if it was a matter of very great urgency, however long the desired system of education may take to see the light of day. Mr. Sargent must know, as an educationist that nowhere in the world the percentage of failures in examinations was fixed beforehand except in India during the British regime.

Mr. Sargent has not taken the trouble of giving any definite scheme to the country which pays him so much and in spite of the fact that he took so much help from so many committees appointed for the purpose. How could he do this unless he was honestly interested in the education of this country? He has put it off by saying, "As already has been pointed out, it will be for the various authorities entrusted with the administration of education at its different stages to work out detailed schemes suited to the particular needs of the areas or institutions for which they are responsible." From these remarks it appears as if all the different areas of India and her institutions had diametrically opposite objectives, ideologies and plans. Some areas sought enlightenment, health and prosperity for themselves and others were after ignorance, disease and poverty; and these authorities alone had responsibilities to discharge while Mr. Sargent, as Educational Adviser to the Government of India, had none! Given the attitude of Mr. Sargent, and the quality of his report, one might as well have entrusted the task to the pupils of any school to frame a system of education for themselves.

Maulana Azad, the Union Minister for Education might have some such system on his anvil which might have kept him busy for the last ten years. The education and national language problem of the country cannot go ahead, he (Maulana Azad) says, for want of books in Hindi and other subjects. Will the books in Hindi and other subjects fall from heavens on some auspicious morning? Isn't it high time that the educational authorities, true to the salt they eat, started working and organizing all this work on sound lines and fixed up Text Book Committees for different subjects on an all-India basis and put their heart honestly into their work? Or, they may leave this work also, like the framing of the system of education for India, to the pupils of some school! Mere signing of routine papers in the office is no work and it requires no special talents. That work could easily be done by any man with the help of a cheap rubber stamp costing a few *annas* only, if per chance he cannot sign papers with his hand. Formerly, during the initial years of India's independence, the excuse put forward by the educational authorities for the lack of material progress in the education of the country was the scarcity of finance. Now that the country has put the necessary finance at the disposal of the Education Minister the anxiety now is how to spend it. Maulana Azad has invited quite recently all Education Ministers of various States to a meeting and some persons among them might come to his help and relieve him of the anxiety. Things seem to be thoroughly rotten in the Education Department of India!

With a view to sugarcoat his bitter pill in the form of the introductory remarks, showing the aims and scope of his work, and with a view to win over the tender sex (approximately 50% of the total population of India) to his side Mr. Sargent comes forward as an advocate of girls' education and teaches us the importance of their education by way of lip-service only, without giving us any scheme for their actual educational betterment.

After discouraging and confusing the country in so many ways he plays the role of a friend of India and ends by advising the country to be up and doing otherwise India will be numbered among the backward nations! We should be thankful to him for this piece of precious advice!

The rest of the Report, covering twelve chapters based, perhaps, mostly on the reports of the different committees appointed from time to time on important matters to be dealt with under education, contains much useful information regarding details for the different stages of education. But the matters concerning the educational policy, the basic principles governing the foundations of education, the medium of instruction, the broad outlines of the superstructure covering the interplay of the technical and scientific with the liberal education at the appropriate ages of school children, and to accommodate the same in school timetable, are much more important than these details. Such important issues are either omitted from the Introduction or a definite wrong lead has been given to the country regarding them and efforts have been made to introduce several poisonous elements in the proposals which will go a long way to disrupt India politically, weaken her economically and strategically.

After inviting the attention of my country towards the Introduction of the said Report and the lead which Mr. Sargent has given to free India in educational matters I would like to discuss very briefly some of the principles of the Wardha Scheme and their future possibilities in the proposed set-up of the Report.

Mahatma Gandhi, it appears, was so overwhelmed by the gigantic nature of the task of education of a big country like India, with huge expenditure involved year after year on the one hand and the stark poverty and unemployment of the masses on the other, that he apparently yielded in despair to the immediate needs upon the country's immediate needs at the cost of promoting education, viz., the resolution of the bread problem first; after all it was one of the basic needs of a seething mass of humanity living in the five hundred and fifty thousand villages of India. He also suggested turning schools into a nucleus for the old professional style guild system[69] by imparting specialized training in arts and crafts, along with a little bit of cultural instruction, and as much of scientific knowledge as might be possible under the circumstances. But that might have given an impetus to a limited number of trades and crafts in the countryside and mofussil towns while providing temporary relief and employment to a section of the country's vast population. The scheme might have been suitable a century or two ago when India was leading an isolated life surrounded by the high Himalayas and the vast seas and when other countries were very backward in education and trade. New developments in science and technology have made India an integral part of the world system. In this machine age, with ever-changing methods of production through research work and scientific knowledge, and cutting down of costs of production, our industries cannot flourish for long and stand world competition without revolutionizing their methods of production along modern lines – for which relevant education is necessary. Moreover, the demands of modern industry and defense need the building up of a strong base and reservoir of skills through a highly developed and broad-based technical and scientific educational

117

superstructure which is not possible under Mahatma Gandhi's proposal. This proposal, therefore, would not have solved the unemployment problem of India and also the problem of her strategic defense on permanent basis. It would have thwarted the full development and growth of the national talent pool and intellectual wealth due to inadequate education, which would have hit hard the material progress of the country in several directions. The field of industry also would have been considerably narrowed down leading to more unemployment and the consequent lowering of the national standards of living, the flooding of our markets with better quality but cheap foreign goods and also to the neglect of the material resources and manpower of the country. This would have resulted in her economic breakdown without full modernization of our education. And, needless to say, without optimum industrialization of the country and full modernization of our industries and agriculture, the military might and strategic security of the country cannot be ensured. In the present international setting, when some of the nations are armed to the teeth and the air is thick with military alliances and pacts, neglect of proper defensive measures would be nothing short of national *hara-kiri*.

As regards the building up of an elaborate system of education around crafts I think it is not fully practicable; moreover its economic spinoffs in the form of poverty alleviation are limited in scope. According to the proposals of the said Report also "basic education, in view of its emphasis on craftwork and the correlation of other subjects therewith, demands a high level of teaching skill", (and also a very highly developed imagination and all round education on the part of teachers, which will not be possible under the Wardha Scheme itself) "if it is to be really successful". Secondly a big country like India requires more than a million teachers at least; and the training of such a large number of teachers to such a high pitch of excellence would have been a utopian dream.

Thirdly the science of education has not developed so far to the extent that it should be able to draw out for our schoolchildren all modern sciences and arts and crafts and numerous other subjects which have beautified and completed modern education, along with elements of culture and morality, from each craft which a child handles, to enable us to supersede the current conventional methods and practices of education which have been followed with success by all advanced countries of the world. Of course, we can liberally change some of the current methods of teaching and rules followed so far so that the student's time is not wasted and the state's money too is utilized to optimum levels in order to satisfy all the four intellectual, moral, physical and vocational requirements of the school, as recommended by Gandhiji for his education through activity, in order to meet the full needs of the nation.

The fact that, in spite of some good admirers among educationists for education through craft, no advanced university or country of the world has so far adopted it practically. This is a clear proof of its impracticability and limitations (If we try to build education around crafts several fields of knowledge will have to be left unexplored since these are more theoretical than practical in nature – poetry and other literary activities for example.). Of course, mere bookish or literary education that has been going on in India so far is worse than useless as far as acquiring tangible creative skills and nation-building efforts are concerned.

The present High School teaching should be broad-based. In fact these ought to be converted into Polytechnic High Schools (PHS) where technical, scientific and industrial education may be given in a four-year course, side by side with liberal education, in order to turn students into good polished citizens culturally as well as professionally so that they are enabled to chart out confidently their independent and decent vocational careers in life. After graduating from the PHS students can go in for specialization/higher studies in a full-fledged polytechnic, college and university. Polytechnic High Schools may be located in District Headquarters and should be fully equipped to provide practical knowledge in technical and scientific work; these should have well equipped libraries, hostels for outstation students, scientific research stations and laboratories etc. To avoid wastage of money every state should be treated as a complete unit for the teaching of technical, scientific and industrial education, which may be distributed in all district headquarters in a planned manner in order to avoid unnecessary duplication. Since every state will not be able to provide skills for every industry there should be provisions for smooth interstate movements of students seeking education in the polytechnic, college or university of their choice.

Literary education must be imparted in tandem with technical education in the syllabus and routine of polytechnic high schools, thus providing joyful activity and a sort of interesting as well as meaningful diversion to the school going child's mind. Theory and practice should be harmoniously interwoven in order to develop the intellect; this would provide suitably skilled labor for various industries, research scholars and teachers for modern sciences, as well as professionals in various arts and crafts. Our industries must seek light from modern scientific theory and research work, which in turn ought to be continuously upgraded in order to keep their practical applications viable as well as profitable.

This is what I have suggested in my proposed system: Theoretical work in the morning is followed by practical or technical work in the afternoon for two hours daily. Students could acquire school-level skills of their choice by choosing from different types of vocations and industries, viz., agriculture, small scale and village industries, mechanics, dairy farming and cattle breeding etc. Every effort ought to be made to take assistance from all modern sciences and technology to make the knowledge of each craft interesting and perfect in every way.

In order to make educational institutions self-supporting, to some extent, which Mahatma Gandhi desired so much, I have proposed in my system of education that two school farms (each of 15 acres) may be allotted by the government to each rural basic school, one for teaching agriculture and the other for teaching dairy farming and cattle rearing. School children will get raw material for these school based industries; moreover milk, butter, fruits, vegetables and rations could also be had for free from these farms' produce. This should ensure good health for the school going children and, therefore, the nation. Since they will be participating in healthy academic as well as practical activities at school the nation will have well rounded youth to further boost progress with the help of a sound technical base. Since they will be taught how to grow cash crops, manufacture cloth and other articles in their school workshop, the students will be able to generate revenue for the school too. This, coupled with instilling the ideals of diligence, self-help, and cooperative habits among students, would help reduce the financial burden of the state to some extent.

I have further tried to cut down the expenses of education by reducing to one half the required number of teachers by introducing new methods of education with the use of magic lantern, educational films, television (for history, geography and Hindi) and radio set etc.

Some more points to note in the Report

Leaving school at the age of eleven years

The Second Wardha Committee of the Central Board of Education has recommended this parting of the ways at the age of eleven plus, which is unscientific and cruel and would cause a lot of heart burning and unrest within the country's student community. 'Abilities', 'aptitudes', and 'general promise' cannot be fully gauged at this age; the weight of all modern educational thought and practice is against it. There is no doubt that a child's interest starts at about 12 years of age but his education should continue without a break or switchover for some time more, i.e. up to 14 years of age at least, so that the child may be able to select the line of his interest more intelligently. This would enable the teachers to give more accurate opinion to the pupil or his guardian in this connection based on longer observation and study of the child. Earlier tendencies of children showing interests or bias in certain directions are of ephemeral character and are sometimes based on passing whims or transient attraction towards novelty and are therefore not authentic or genuine. Secondly, examination marks are no certain and unerring criteria for deciding a child's potential and merit. It has been often seen that students occupying top positions in examinations have proved horrible failures in life and the so called mediocre ones in schools have sometimes occupied top positions in practical life. So, obviously, the present system of evaluating a child's potential is flawed.

The report contains the weaknesses of its own suggestion that selection of pupils be made at the age of 11 for high school admission "by requiring special arrangements to be made for the transfer from Senior Basic (middle) Schools to High Schools of suitable children and particularly those who show signs of late development." Then why should we not make this selection of all pupils at the end of the Senior Basic Education without causing unnecessary heart burning and disappointment to 80% children of the country who will think that they have been mercilessly caught by the neck and thrown overboard against their own and their guardians' wishes without any cogent justification? Further, in the chapter on Technical, Commercial and Art Education, the Report says "that the first three years of the course will be mainly devoted to general subjects." Then why this desperate hurry in parting of the ways at the early age of 11? Why not give general education, mixed with technical education, in Senior Basic in the afternoon session in order to create a sound base for industry, agriculture, arts, sciences and mechanics? This would provide proper opportunity to all children of the country to confidently choose the class of professional activity they want to take up for the rest of their lives. By this unscientific selection for the High School and the University, the higher education in India will be further cut down and all constructive work and industrial progress of the country will get a serious setback. India is already the most backward amongst the advanced nations of the world in university education. As the Report would have it, in pre-War Germany the proportion of students in the universities to the entire population was 1 to 690, in Great Britain it was 1 to 857, in the United States 1 to 225, in Russia 1 to 300, while in India it is 1 to 2206". Does the Central Advisory Board of Education mean to reduce it still further?

High Schools in rural areas

Considering the infrastructure and resources at the country's disposal, the proposal for setting up High Schools with hostels and conveyance arrangements in villages is uneconomical. This will also cause the lowering of educational standards. All High Schools, like Polytechnic Institutes, should be in district headquarters and it should be so planned that every village has easy access to these schools by road. The report assumes again 50% of the High Schools with hostels and conveyance arrangements in rural areas. If most of the pupils of High Schools in rural areas are to live in hostels, and conveyance arrangements are also to be provided for the pupils' daily travel to and from distant villages, (for one village possessing such a school cannot make up the required number of pupils for the school), why should not these High Schools be established only in District Headquarters with the residential system and hostel accommodation for pupils coming from rural areas where no daily conveyance arrangement will be necessary and where they will have comprehensive facilities for all types of education? This will help save the students' time and prevent unnecessary expenditure by the State. These facilities cannot be made available in all rural areas. Moreover, the rural areas cannot afford a sufficient number of pupils to make a good polytechnic high school with a high standard of education. Further, Technical High Schools in rural areas cannot afford separate high-level classes, laboratories, big industrial workshops and staff of specialists, museums, meteorological stations, libraries and experimental stations of their own for the use of students. Hence the suggestion of having all these resources at the district headquarters which should be equidistant for all students.

Sir John Sargent's recommendations on medium of instruction in High Schools

The Board further proposes the medium of instruction in all High Schools to be the (provincial) mother tongue of the pupil. Have they ever contemplated the long term effects of the proposal? Would Mr. Sargent propose the Welsh language in the schools of Wales, the Scotch language in the schools of Scotland and the Irish language similarly in the schools of Northern Ireland? They further propose that English should be the compulsory second language! How long will it take us to shake off this mental slavery and the old ruts? Why not standard English books on different subjects be translated into Hindi or new books written in Hindi, based on the consolidated knowledge, for the benefit of school children rather than ask them all to master the foreign English language first, so that they may understand their different subjects? This takes away their attention from other subjects, which they could easily master in Hindi and in less time. They are asked in the scheme for academic High School to master the mother tongue (provincial language), English and other classical and modern languages and they are considered suitable subjects for study while the national language, which alone, among other things, will make the system 'national' has been left out. Are all of our pupils to be made linguists at the cost of other subjects and also at the cost of true education and health? Let us have separate arrangements in different parts of the country for the teaching of foreign languages, and modern and classical languages for the benefit of those pupils who want to avail of such opportunities rather than compel the entire student world to pass through that narrow needle's eye at the cost of their time and health. In the scheme for Technical High Schools, similarly, the mother tongue (provincial language), English, classical languages and modern languages are recommended but the national language, Hindi, is again missing. In my opinion no other language in High Schools, as medium of instruction, is required except Hindi. In the case of pure 'academic' group of pupils the second compulsory language should be Sanskrit and no other. There should be separate schools for all other languages, classical or non-classical, for those who want to take up those courses after completing the Secondary course.

Disparity in teachers' pay-scales

There is, again, too much disparity between the scales of pay of teachers on the one hand and of Headmasters and Headmistresses on the other. This wide gap should also be narrowed down to legitimate/fair limits if socialistic pattern of society is our aim.

Number of pupils in a High School Class

Again, in the High Schools, one teacher for twenty pupils is too big a luxury for poor India, especially in the initial stages. The Report says: "one teacher for 20 pupils may be taken as a suitable staffing formula". Is this formula used for all classes in Britain whose expenditure per head of population is the equivalent of Rs. 33/2 against India having only annas 8/9 per head of population as mentioned by Mr. Sargeant in his report?

Polytechnic Institutes

The Report of C.A.B suggests separate establishment of junior technical institutions and senior technical institutions. This will prove to be uneconomical and derogatory to the smooth, harmonious and graded development of technical education in the country. It will necessitate duplication of our scarce resources like the specialist staff needed for workshops and laboratories, as well as of workshop and laboratory assistants, of equipment and management. Why not create separate classes in the continued Polytechnic Institutes for different grades of students/workers with different periods of studies, and different educational qualifications of the entrants as given below?

It is suggested that only higher engineering and technology of the higher university level courses may be taught separately at special Heavy Industry Centers but all under the control of the University of the State concerned as all technical education should be necessarily under the university's control.

Technical course in Polytechnic Institutes

(a) One year's fulltime apprenticeship course after completing Senior Basic Course (Certificate to be granted after examination);

(b) Two to three years' fulltime technical course after senior basic course (Certificate to be granted after examination);

(c) Four years (afternoon classes) part time technical course for high school students (Certificate to be granted after examination);

(d) Two years' further full time technician's course for the above category after completing secondary course (Diploma to be granted after examination).

In technical colleges

Four to five years' fulltime course for higher technology or engineering should be conducted after secondary course at technical colleges. This should be at selected units of heavy and large scale Industrial Centers in order to produce graduates in technology and engineering (Degrees B.Sc. Tech and B.Sc. Engineering to be granted after examination).

Teachers and buildings for adult education

No special teachers or special buildings are necessary for adult education as proposed in the Report, for that will be sheer waste of money. The school buildings and equipment, educational films, magic lanterns, radio sets etc, when available, can be used for the education of adults too. The school staff, with the help of

126

properly organized local voluntary effort and pupil teachers, may teach the adults and they (teachers) may be given extra 10% of their salary as Adult Education Allowance for this work. They may be suitably trained in the Teachers' Training Colleges to enable them to handle this additional work. To cut down costs of education and to revolutionize education the manufacture of cine projectors, educational films in Hindi, magic lanterns with slides and radio sets should be taken in hand at once and on a very large scale too. Several factories should be started in different places for the purpose and all the 300[70] districts or so of India should be supplied with those educational instruments every month in some regular order till all schools – urban and rural – are provided with these materials. With the help of publicity girls could be encouraged to train as teachers, nurses and midwives as the next step forward.

Nucleus for Teachers' Training Centers

For the Second Five Year Plan period (1956-1961), which would in fact be the first five year plan period for education, we require a very large number of lady teachers for Kindergartens and junior basic classes (Standards I to IV). Every state, therefore, should organize in all District Headquarters one such nucleus for the training of girls and women for the teaching work for the said classes. These centers should be attached to the local Kindergartens and junior basic schools in District Headquarters where the trainees should take three months' theoretical and one month's practical training for teaching work just after the third term. These classes should be opened during the vacations, three times a year, and each term should consist of one month only. Thus three months' theoretical training in one year followed by a month's practical training should be considered enough in the initial stages. This should be followed by refresher courses on Sundays for another year for further instruction and to remove practical difficulties of the trained staff. These classes for teachers' training should be carried on with the help of all trained teachers. All such trained teachers should be conscripted for the purpose as a form of national compulsory service in rotation for five years period. In these training centers and in the refresher courses, the trainees should also be given guidance on how to handle the adult education. Residential facilities should be given to all trainees who come from rural areas and free food facilities to deserving cases. The states should appeal to the patriotic feelings of the female population to come out and serve the country at the time of her special need, according to their capacity or education, and enroll themselves for training as teachers, nurses and midwives etc. This would also improve their financial condition and secure economic independence for them. The local Congress organizations can play a beautiful role in this respect by attracting the woman population of India to these noble professions. After the three months of training during vacations, followed by one month's practical course, all the trained hands should be engaged by the state on attractive pay-scales and detailed on duty. In filling vacancies in schools preference may be given, as far as possible, to local people and couples. Similarly schemes should be handled in district hospitals for the training of nurses and midwives on regular basis. After the Second Five Year Plan period (1956-1961) is over, there should be enough Teachers' Training Colleges to be started in the country for the training of teachers for senior basic and high school classes.

The order of precedence in education

The plan of education as approved by the Education Board is proposed to be tried area by area. I think it may be more in the fitness of things if, instead of pursuing the plan area to area or exactly even from age to age, it is worked on the basis of 'first things first'. On the one hand we should not delay laying correct foundations of education; on the other hand we must not delay meeting the very urgent needs of the nation in the present context. During the second Five Year Plan period (1956-1961) it would be advisable to concentrate on nurseries, Kindergartens and junior basic (after four standards only) on free and compulsory basis.

Further, the central government may take up the organization of some polytechnic institutes at important centers for the training of various categories of skilled workers for our heavy industry along with the training of lady teachers, nurses and midwives. Adult education too may be imparted to the extent possible under the circumstances. At the top of the pyramid it is essential to train lady doctors (both physicians and surgeons) as well as to concentrate on scientific research work and the training of persons for higher technology and engineering, with hands-on experience at the units of heavy and large scale industries.

From time to time it would be essential to carry out fine-tuning and updating in the methods, or courses of instruction, of conducting senior basic and high school classes in the light of new proposed arrangements. During the Third Five Year plan period (1961-1966), the organization of the senior basic and high school classes may be similarly taken up on free and compulsory basis up to the end of senior basic course. Teachers Training Colleges need to be set up on a large scale for the training of senior basic and high school class teachers as also for further extension of more efficient training arrangements of lady teachers for Kindergartens and the junior basic classes, as well as for more nurses, midwives and lady doctors (Physicians and Surgeons). At the top we may need to further concentrate upon the extension of the schemes for scientific research work and higher technology and engineering. During this interval again efforts may be made to make minor adjustments in further crystallizing and extending the scope of the different faculties and to bring them in line with some of the advanced western universities. During the Fourth Five Year Plan period (1966-1971) we may concentrate upon modernizing our university education to the full, facilitating maximum development of technology, engineering and all sciences and arts; this is also the period when various adult education programs should conclude successfully. By the end of this period there should be no scarcity of teachers, nurses, midwives and doctors and the country should also be self-sufficient to meet all her needs within the country for technicians and all kinds of machinery. Thus, India could be standing on her legs in the field of education within fifteen years from now instead of waiting for forty long years as promised by Sir John Sargent.

Conclusion

From the above long history of Indian education one may draw the following conclusions:

1) India is a country whose system of education has been the oldest in the world; and its teaching was based on the four *Vedas* which are the fountain-head of all basic knowledge – spiritual and material – and essentially cover all, what have come to be known as, modern disciplines like philosophy, arts and sciences.

2) A very long chain of institutions imparting education shine like so many light posts from age to age, from the very ancient *Vedic* period right up to the occupation of India by Britain.

3) During the *Sutra* period the standard of education was remarkably high. It attracted students even from foreign countries. It was also broad-based covering the spiritual, the moral, the intellectual, the physical and the technical aspects of a student's development.

4) In India there was a serious setback to education during the Muslim rule no doubt. However, the sacred fire of enlightenment was kept burning even in those stormy and dark centuries – no matter how dim the light it emitted sometimes.

5) The indigenous education system in India further deteriorated during the British regime as the British Government of India destroyed the Indian village system with which it had enjoyed certain degree of symbiosis. Further, communal poison was injected into the educational superstructure and its scope was narrowed down considerably in order to serve the imperial interests and those of the British trade and industry.

6) The superstructure of education, both in the ancient and the medieval systems and also in the *Sutra* age before the arrival of Muslim invaders, was built on the genius of the people living in

this great country. In other words the educational base was built according to their national culture covering *Dharma* (moral development), *Artha* (economic or material development), *Kama* (mental and aesthetical development) and *Moksha* (spiritual development). That is to say, the material, mental and aesthetical advancement of the country, as indicated by the development of her occupations, arts, sciences and technology, has always moved forward from age to age with her moral and spiritual advancement in which, of course, the former group served only as a handmaid of the latter.

7) The present Union Ministry of Education (headed by Maulana Azad) as a highly technical department has proved itself entirely inefficient, if not completely dishonest and should therefore be overhauled and the Central Advisory Board of Education also should be reformed, strengthened, specialized and reorganized for reorientation of Indian education and its innumerable activities especially in the fields of national language, national literature, national history, national arts and sciences and in the social life of the nation.

The cultural foundation of the proposed system of education

The national ideology and the way of life should shine from our educational institutions as the sun and the moon shine from the sky. The chief characteristics of the nation i.e. its genius and culture as shown in our inclinations, pursuits, hobbies, traditions, philosophy, past history, and literature couched in the national language, should be as clearly visible through our education as stars during nights. The education should further reflect our arts, sciences and technology. It should be built again on the needs, present and future, of the country. It must cease to be a blind copy of any other system however perfect or beneficial that may appear to be. Then and then only will our system of education be natural to the soil, useful and of permanent value to the country. India must have her roots in herself if she is at all anxious to carve out a beautiful destiny for her progeny and that is possible only by putting her culture or genius in the very foundations of her future system of education.

Appendix - 1

Madrasa education in India: Is it to sustain medieval attitude among Muslims? By R. Upadhyay

A recent circular of Government of India to keep watch on the anti-national activities of madrasas raised many eyebrows in the country. But if we look back to the historical developments of madrasa in India this Islamic system of education has all along been playing a prominent role in keeping the movement of Muslim separatism alive in this country. The British also suspected them. Contrary to it the post-colonial India, for reason best known, gave special constitutional privilege for the autonomy of madrasas. But the manner in which the madrasas promote medieval attitude among Indian Muslims at the cost of secular education needs to be checked. In fact, orthodoxy, religious conservatism and obsession to medieval identity remained the main focus of Madrasa education in India.

Being the lifeline of Muslim society madrasa is the real foundation of Muslim education in India. But in absence of clarity of vision about the present day economic and social needs of Indian Muslims, madrasa managers failed to play a positive role in the scheme of their education and preferred to keep the community subjugated under medieval psyche for their vested political interests.

"Madrasa is an institution of learning, where Islamic sciences including literary and philosophical ones are taught" (Encyclopedia of Islam - Leiden E.J. Brill). Avowed aim of madrasa education is to inculcate the belief and practice of Islam among its followers and guide them to follow Koran and traditions of the Prophet. The foundation of madrasa education is therefore, basically standing on two pillars of Quran (Collection of God's revelations to Prophet Mohammad) and Sunna (Tradition of Prophet Mohammad).

The history of madrasa dates back to the establishment of Delhi Sultanate in 1206 CE Initially its principal function was to train personnel for government service (Encyclopedia of Islam) and accordingly curriculum was formulated to cater to the administrative needs of Muslim rulers. Gradually with the patronage of these rulers it was extended to different parts of north India. The claim of some Muslim thinkers that religious, rational and natural sciences were also introduced in the curriculum of madrasa in India to meet the educational need of the time appears to be a myth. "Science flourished in the Golden Age of Islam because there was within Islam strong rationalist tradition, carried out by a group of Muslim thinkers known as Mutazilites" (Parvez Hoodbhoy quoted in 'The Secularist' in its issue no.191 September-October 2002). This tradition however, collapsed by the 14th century and the Muslim World was "choked in the vice-like grip of orthodoxy" (Ibid).

The organization of madrasa in India and its working all along remained religion-centric. Subjects related to Islam continually dominated its curriculum in India ever since its inception. While carrying forward the legacy of Perso-Arabic educational thought Indian madrasa steadily propagated the conservative outlook and attitude of a larger section of Indian Muslims. Madrasa organizers in India never thought of how far its curriculum would be relevant in the changing environment. Greater importance on theological aspect of Islam in curriculum of Muslim education largely ignored the rational sciences. The religion-based education in these institutions gave birth to bigotry and became a major source of tension in Indian society. There might have been strong rationalist tradition of Islamic education as claimed by Muslim educationists but the madrasas in India failed to keep pace with the fast changing modern social and educational environment.

With the disintegration of Muslim rule, particularly after the advent of British, madrasa education gradually lost its shine it had during the Muslim rule. It received a major setback and suffered further reversal with the introduction of modern education. Madrasa teachers, therefore, became restive and developed a more rigid attitude towards religion-centric education for Muslims. The historic participation of madrasa leaders in 1857 revolt against British regime proved that the main objective of traditional Islamic education was to attune the Indian Muslims with aspiration for regaining of political power. With Ulema playing significant role in the revolt, the British started suspecting madrasas as possible centers of disaffection.

After the failure of 1857revolt Muslim Ulema feared that the Muslim mode of life may got diluted due to the western education introduced by the British. Their immediate need was to keep a check on the possibility of their community moving towards modern education and ensure to carry forward the Persian-Arab legacy, which was possible only through madrasa education. They launched madrasa movement by establishing an Islamic seminary known as Darul Uloom at Deoband in 1866 with a view to educate Indian Muslims with Islamic system of education. By the close of nineteenth century madrasas like Farangi Mahal (Lucknow), Dar-al-Ulum (Deoband) and Nadwat-al-Ulama (Lucknow) emerged as vibrant symbols for Muslim separatist movement in India.

Contrary to Deoband movement Sir Syed Ahmad a British loyalist launched Aligarh movement and "established Madrastul Ulum at Aligarh in 1873 for imparting education in modern branches of learning, which later became Mohammadan Anglo Oriental College and then Aligarh Muslim University" (Education and Muslims in India since Independence edited by A.W.B. Qadri and others, 1998, page81). Being more realistic he tried to inspire Muslim society towards modern education. "Sayed Ahmad Khan, founder of Aligarh Muslim University, found the madrasa syllabus unsuited to the present age and to the spirit of the times. He criticized it for encouraging memorizing rather than real understanding.

The scholar Fazlur Rahman commented: "By organically relating all forms of knowledge and gearing these to dogmatic theology the very sources of intellectual fecundity were blighted and possibility of original thinking stifled" (Mushirul Hasan in Hindu dated May 21, 2003). Even though both the institutions were antithesis of each other their main objective was to keep the movement of Muslim separatism alive.

With a view to fashioning the education policy exclusively for Indian Muslims, Sir Syed Ahmad formed All India Muslim Educational Conference in 1886. It was in fact a part of Aligarh movement. Its basic aim was to fashion the education policy for Indian Muslims and encourage them towards the mainstream of western education. Even today it continues to haunt the community with the ghost of alleged Hindu-biased education in government schools. This attitude of social exclusivism worked as catalyst in fostering Muslim communal consciousness and caused a major damage to Hindu-Muslim unity in the Indian sub-continent. Later it gave birth to the two-nation theory. "Arguably, its contribution to ultimate partition of India, although not greatly evident on the surface of affairs, was not much less great than that of its most famous child, the All India Muslim League" (All India Muslim Educational Conference by Abdul Rasid Khan, 2001, page 251). This shows that a reformist like Sir Syed Ahmad had no vision for India in which both the Hindus and Muslims could have a common education.

Deriving inspiration from both Deoband and Aligarh, other prominent Islamic seminaries like Nadwatul Ulama and Jamia Millia were later established in Lucknow and Delhi respectively. Nadwa introduced rational sciences and working knowledge of English in its courses of study but its over emphasis on Arabic literature and Islamic History did not bring the desired result for its products in job market. Jamia Millia tried to combine Deoband and Aligarh in its educational thought but its religious character and obsession for Urdu language as medium of instruction remained a major obstacle to its recognition as a symbol of modern education.

Due to deep-rooted medieval attitude in the minds of Indian Muslims these Islamic institutions also failed to transform the mindset of their students so that they could think independently for developing a critical perspective and analyzing their lives in a more meaningful manner suited to contemporary global environment. Accordingly Nadwa also remained as conservative as Deoband. Jamia, however, accepted modern education to a considerable extent but its obsession for

Urdu as medium of instruction could not bring its students at par with other modern educational institutions in the country as far as the job market is concerned.

Though a section of Muslim thinkers supported the Aligarh Movement launched by Sir Syed Ahmad as a positive response to western education, the largest majority of Muslim mass supported Deoband movement, which favored Islam centric education. They strongly opposed the Aligarh movement launched by Sir Sayed Ahmad who had tried to inculcate modern and scientific education.

With main objective to propagate Islam, madrasas in India formulated sociopolitical agenda on Perso-Arabic traditions with a view to keep the Muslim community away from the contemporary modern and scientific world. Even the contemporary rationalist Muslim thinkers, who talk about Islamic modernism, have hardly overcome their medieval attitude of intellectual subjugation. They have, in fact, ignored the real problem that how far madrasa education would be relevant in contemporary social advancement of the country. Factually, there is hardly any difference between madrasa education and modern education imparted by Muslim institutions like Aligarh Muslim University as far as the medieval attitude of their students is concerned. Madrasa education, which is basically for propagation of Islam, therefore, always remained an inspiration for modern Muslim educational institutions.

Indian Muslims continue to be obsessed with madrasa education and its Perso-Arabic legacy as a result it is difficult for them to admit that sound and fruitful knowledge also exists in any language other than Arabic and Persian. They cannot think of any knowledge that is not stored in Islamic literatures. Carrying forward the legacy of Perso-Arabic system of education and treating them as Indo-Muslim cultural heritage the madrasas in India played vital role in propagating the ideology of two-nation theory. Partition of the country put similar stigma on madrasas in free India because the largest majority of Muslims in

British India were in favor of partition on the basis of this two-nation theory.

After partition the largest section of educated Muslims migrated to Pakistan. But those who stayed back passed through a state of frustration due their apprehension of likely setback in their movement of Muslim separatism. The future of madrasa education in Hindu dominated secular and democratic Indian polity became an issue of primary concern for them. Their leaders in post-colonial India gave them the wrong impression about alleged Hindu-biased education. Instead of joining hands with Hindus in national reconstruction programs Indian Muslims took up the problem of their separate identity as primary concern and failed to avail the equal opportunity provided to all the Indian citizens under the country's constitution.

Despite the rising tide of anguish of Hindus against Muslims after partition Indian leadership gave constitutional protection to Muslims for managing their educational institutions. Despite this some who stayed back in India sensed a danger to their cultural identity.

Taking advantage of Indian constitution providing the minorities with special privilege for establishing their educational institutions, there was a spurt in expansion of madrasa education in India. Accordingly Qazi Mohammad Abdul Abbasi, a senior Congress leader with the support of madrasa leaders organized Deeni Talimi Council in Uttar Pradesh in December 1959 with a view to establish maqtab (Primary school) for imparting the fundamentals of Islam to every Muslim student at primary level. The council was formed "to fight against what was perceived as Hindu-based education being imparted in various government schools" (Madrasa Education in India - Kuldip Kaur, 1990, page 203). Abbasi, while addressing the Deeni Council in Banaras in 1960, said:

"I am of the opinion that we must not seek any government help for this Deeni Talimi Council and must not associate ourselves with the educational department of the government" (Ibid, page 204). Poor response of Muslims to government schools was due to their notion that the education imparted in these schools was against the tradition of Islam.

Managers of madrasas, while remaining inflexible and maintaining the Islamic traditions and culture, never gave any thought to job opportunities for the products of madrasa education. Even Islamic institutions like Deoband and Nadwa, which had maintained strategic opposition to partition of the country, hardly made any change in their courses of study and method of teaching even after Independence. They have produced thousands of graduates and established a large number of madrasas over the years but did not provide them an opportunity for the material progress. They are, therefore, equally responsible for the material plight of the Indian Muslims and for their economic, social and educational backwardness as we see today.

Contrary to the secular education system formulated in India after Independence madrasas were promoted as major obstacles for Indian Muslims in taking the benefit of utilitarian concept of education, which is basically for the material progress of Indian society. They inculcated among Indian Muslims an obsession for education in purely Islamic environment, which kept them off from government schools. Thus, growth of maqtab and madrasas in different parts of the country also served as nucleus for sustaining a full-fledged movement in retaining a separate Muslim identity.

"Today there are lakhs of Madrasas spread all over the country" (Indian Muslims by Maulana Wahiduddin Khan, page 88) which, however, could not enlighten Indian Muslims to develop a positive outlook." Though a section of the Muslim elite entered into the field of modern education they could not inspire the common Muslims who remained under the subjugation of the fundamentalists within the community. They are still obsessed with Islamic interpretation of education by conservative Muslims. "The ultimate aim of Muslim education lies in the realization of complete submission to Allah on the level of the individual, the community and humanity at large"

(New Horizons in Muslim Education by S.A. Asraf, 1985, page 4).

One can understand the reaction of Indian Muslims against the Western system of education introduced by the British after the collapse of Muslim rule in India because they were deprived of political power. But, after Independence, if the Muslims who stayed back in India voluntarily remained obsessed with their traditional Islamic education system they cannot blame anyone except their own leadership for their educational backwardness. If they still enjoy remaining under the subjugation of radical Islamists no one can stop them from slipping rapidly down the educational and economic scale.

Conclusion

Whether Madrasa education has led to the decline of educational or economic position of Indian Muslims in present environment may be a debatable issue, but that its Islam-centric teaching is not friendly to the job market in the contemporary world is the ground reality. In the absence of modern knowledge the graduates produced by madrasas are neither able to improve their own material prosperity nor they provide leadership to the Muslim community to face the challenge of modern world. Their job opportunity is restricted to mosques and madrasas. Even for higher Islamic studies the degrees awarded by madrasas are not recognized by Indian universities except in the theological department of Aligarh Muslim University and Jamia Millia. Similarly, such degrees are not recognized for administrative jobs in the government. Since these degrees are not market friendly they do not have any practical value.

Without any concern for the material progress of Indian Muslims madrsas are only producing Islamic zealots so that they could remain loyal to Islam and to the political interest of Muslim community. Emphasis on Islamic education at the cost of secular education is detrimental to the national interest.

In view of the ongoing changes in the social, cultural, economic, and political environment drastic change is required in madrasa system of education so that Indian Muslims could come to terms with the changing needs of the contemporary Indian society. The feeling among Indian Muslims that government and public schools are loaded with learning related to Hindu culture is to be changed so that Muslim parents could send their children in those schools without hesitation. But the Muslim leaders and thinkers, barring a couple of exceptions, are so much bogged down with the political problems of their community that they are not found assertive enough on their modern educational problem, which is the real issue.

A section of Muslim thinkers are in favor of modernization of madrasa education and transforming them according to the present day needs. But they hardly oppose the radical Islamists, who suggest that "instead of turning Islamic madrasas into English or modern institutions, the modern educational institutions be made Muslim" (Education and Muslims in India since Independence - Edited by A.W.B. Qadri, 1998, page85).

Memorization of Islamic scriptures without any rational understanding befitting the contemporary cultural and social environment may not serve the real purpose of education. Concerned with the economic backwardness of their community Muslim rationalists might have a genuine desire to free the community from the academic bondage of madrasa education but the task is very difficult due to the firm grip of fundamentalist forces over the community. It is a fact that Indian madrasas have produced a number of world famous Islamic scholars, but lakhs of Muslim educated from theses madrasas are deprived of the job opportunities because of their ignorance of modern knowledge.

Madrasa managers might have their own arguments in support of their theological command but keeping off the Muslims with the realities of contemporary world has caused immense harm to the community as far as its economic development is concerned. Curriculum of madrasa ignored the sociology of religion and did not allow any independent thinking on the plea that Islam is a comprehensive, perfect and complete way of life for all the times. In the absence of the clarity of vision about the contemporary social environment in India madrasa education failed to secularize the behavior of the Muslim society with social enlightenment.

The madrasa system of education was basically meant for preparing the people for Islamic way of life and Islamization of all the branches of knowledge even though the contemporary world does not accept it as a sole criterion of education. Theological education, which is a specialized subject, needs segregation from the education for the contemporary worldly needs. But, ironically, Indian Muslims are not ready to accept it because their orthodox religious obsession and fear of losing cultural identity has pushed them into isolation.

Educational backwardness of Indian Muslims is a national problem. But so long they do not respond to the remedial measures it is difficult to be resolved. The country should be ready to extend them a helping hand if and when they come forward and make a conscious endeavor to transform their madrasas into modern educational institutions with Islamic subjects as optional courses.

(E-mail <ramashray60 @rediffmail.com>)

Note: The permission to include this article was granted by Mr. R. Upadhyay vide his email dated 20 May 2009.

Appendix - 2

Muslims and education By Dr. Asghar Ali Engineer

It is generally thought that Muslims do not prefer to send their children, especially girl-child, to school. They are mainly concerned about religious education and therefore are inclined to open more and more madrasas. This stereotype was further reinforced when in mid-seventies number of madrasas were opened, especially in northern, western and central India. This was mainly because it was in early seventies that oil revolution took place in the Arab world and they began to give money to poorer Muslim countries including for religious education. Many Ulama from India succeeded in getting financial aid for starting new madrasas and also expanding existing madrasas. It is undoubtedly true that during seventies and in subsequent decades quite a few madrasas were established in India.

However, there are many reasons for expansion of madrasas, which must be understood. It should not be reduced to a stereotype, which is often done. First, we would like to throw some light on the prevalence of madrasa education among Muslims in India. Firstly, it should be noted that during Muslim rule in medieval ages these madrasas were centers of higher knowledge and these madrasas provided religious as well as then available scientific knowledge known as 'ulum-i-aqliyah' (intellectual knowledge). These centers of learning were naturally patronized by the kings, nawabs and jagirdars (feudal lords). Thus what is known as Dars-i-Nizamiyah synthesized both religious and natural sciences of the time.

However, with the decline of the Mughal rule and establishment of British rule these centers of higher knowledge fast declined and were left with no resources to grow and imbibe the modern knowledge. Now small madrasas came into existence in different localities, which were run by donations from local communities and catered to elementary religious knowledge. The biggest institution of Islamic learning which

145

came into existence in the post-Mughal period in north India was Darul 'Ulum Deoband. This institution founded by Maulana Qasim Ahmed Nanotvi and others also had very humble beginnings. It was founded in nineteenth century after the failure of the 1857 war of independence.

This madrasa had come into existence during a period of great crisis for north Indian Muslims when Muslims were facing British wrath and the 'Ulama were in the forefront of anti-British struggle much before the Indian national Congress came into existence and national freedom movement started. These 'Ulama remained steadfast in their struggle for freedom and also became allies of the Congress and firmly opposed the two nation theory and partition of the country. These 'Ulama led by Maulana Mahmudul Hasan opposed modern education not so much because it was modern and secular but more so as it was a British imperialist system.

Sir Syed on the other hand became founder of the modern educational institution in Aligarh known as MAO College, which subsequently became Aligarh Muslim University. In a way both Sir Syed and the Ulama of Deoband School were complementing each other rather than contradicting. Both systems of education were needed in that period of acute crisis. It was, for Muslims, also a period of acute identity crisis. Modern secular education alone would not have sufficed for Muslims during that period of crisis. It was very difficult for the Muslim elite to come to terms with total eclipse of their power. And it was for this reason the 'Ulama played far more significant role in freedom struggle to drive the British out than the secular Muslim elite. The secular elite were far more interested in making a deal with the Britishers to safeguard their own interests.

The 'Ulama at the same time were more worried about religious identity and hence madrasa education flourished under their patronage. Also, it was in keeping with the requirement of Muslims as there was glaring poverty among them since most of them were converted from lower Hindu castes. Modern western education made not much sense to them nor could they afford it as they faced stark poverty. Many sociologists have pointed out that among Indian Muslims before independence there was either feudal class or the poor class. Thus either there were very rich Muslims (mostly from feudal class) or very poor Muslims, middle class being very weak. The 'Ulama catered to the poorer classes by opening madrasas where free religious education was imparted and many madrasas also offered free food and clothing.

The period immediately after partition was also full of crisis for Muslims. The educated rich and middle classes migrated to Pakistan for greener pastures and poor illiterate masses were left behind. Once again it was madrasa education which came to their rescue and fulfilled their psychological and intellectual need. The Government of India could not open even enough primary schools to fulfill the need for schooling for the poor. Muslims, being among the extremely poor, had to fall back on the madrasa education. And those who somehow could make it to government schools dropped out before completing primary education as the poor parents would like them to work somewhere to supplement family income. But even after dropping out they would continue madrasa education due to convenient timings – either early morning or late evening.

All this put together accounts for lack of secular education among the Muslims and flourishing of madrasa education. The 'Ulama also saw an opportunity to run more madrasas after oil revolution and many more madrasas came into existence including those of higher learning which catered to increased Muslim population in the post-independence period. Now, girls also began to join both primary and higher centers of Islamic learning. There are courses being run for girls in places like Malegaon in Maharashtra and other places.

However, having said this about the madrasa education, I would like to discuss the situation about the modern secular education. It is necessary to dispel the stereotype that Muslims resist modern secular education and opt for madrasa education only. Such stereotypes, besides being unreal, are also dangerous as they intensify communal attitudes. Madrasas are looked upon as centers of fundamentalism and also now generally dubbed as centers of ISI activities. This is, to say the least, highly politically motivated. It is highly regrettable that Mr. Advani announced that madrasa education is a security risk. Mr. Advani and his intelligence services should know better. There may be a few black sheep but such sweeping statements are very dangerous and amount to condemning the whole community. Those, which indulge in such activities should be isolated and punished under the law of the land.

Apart from madrasa education there is a growing trend today among Muslims to go for secular education. So far the socio-cultural factors rather than religious ones kept Muslim girls away from modern school education. Today, with the growth of middle class among the Muslims, the trend for modern education is on the rise. This year, for example, a Muslim girl Nuashin Khan topped in B.Sc. from Bombay University. Another Muslim girl from Bihar obtained second position in the IAS examination. According to 1981 survey there are 0.4% graduates now among Muslims. Compared to others it may appear as a dismal figure but, nevertheless, it shows changing trends among Muslims.

According to a survey in U.P. by Mr. Sherwani the number of Muslim girls passing matriculation in first class has jumped 13 times. Though the base may not be very high still the jump of 13 percent is no mean figure. The same survey by Nusrat and Ahmed Rashid Sherwani indicates that in different colleges in U.P. there is great increase in the success rate of Muslim girls. Also, all over India, one finds increasing number of Muslim colleges, particularly girl colleges, coming into existence. It is a highly encouraging trend. Syed Hamid, ex-Vice Chancellor of Aligarh Muslim University, has taken it as his life's mission to popularize modern secular education among Muslims. He had taken out a Talimi Caravan (educational caravan) through various cities and towns of north India to urge upon Muslims to go for modern education. It has had considerable impact on the Muslim mind.

There is a great difference between stereotypes and ground reality. While the stereotype remains static the ground reality changes. Muslims are still very backward as all social, economic and educational indicators bear out. Yet, the new middleclass, which is emerging on the Muslim horizon, is realizing that the community must advance in educational field in this information technology era. Azim Premji, the only high ranking industrialist among Muslims in India has declared that his foundation will educate 60 thousand students every year and he also declared that education is the best gift one can give to children.

The Government of India, under the premiership of Mr. Rao, had announced to give Rs.500 crores to Maulana Azad Foundation for educational and other needs of the community. However, the government gave only Rs. 100 crores. The Congress Party in Maharashtra had promised Rs.100 crores for Muslims in its election manifesto. However, it has given only Rs. 5 crores so far. If the government fulfils its promises Muslims can achieve much higher rate of literacy. The main problem for education among Muslims is poverty, not religion or lack of will. There are not many industrialists or businessmen among Indian Muslims like Azim Premji to come to their rescue. Now there seems to be a will among Muslims but no resources. There is also a trend for imparting modern education in the madrasas. But again the lack of resources stares in the face of Muslims. Some madrasas have, however, adopted modern sciences as part of their curriculum.

Note: The permission to include this article was granted by Dr. Asghar Ali Engineer vide his email dated 21 May 2009.

NOTES

_____

[1] Jauhar, originally, meant voluntary self-immolation on a funeral pyre by queens and royal womenfolk of defeated Rajput kingdoms. The term has been extended to describe the occasional practice of mass suicide carried out in medieval times by Rajput women and men. Mass self-immolation by women was called *Jauhar*. This was usually done before or at the same time their menfolk rode out in a charge to meet their attackers and certain death. The upset caused by the knowledge that their women and younger children were dead, no doubt, filled them with rage in this fight to the death called *saka*. – Ed.

[2] Lala Hardayal was a revolutionary and a scholar who dedicated himself to the cause of Indian Freedom. He was the Gadar Party's General Secretary and was a prominent leader in the Gadar movement. He traveled to many parts of the world and helped to spread the idea of the freedom movement.

Lala was born on October 14, 1884 at Delhi. He secured Masters in English Literature from the Government College of Lahore. He was awarded a State Scholarship by the Government of India to study at Oxford, England. While in England he became involved with the Indian struggle for freedom.

In England he came in close contact with revolutionaries and reformers like C.F. Andrews, S.K. Verma and Bhai Permanand. He vehemently protested against the British oppression of Indians and resigned from his scholarship. He returned to India and dedicated himself to political activities in Lahore. He left family life to adopt the life of a monk. During this period he contributed articles to the Modern Review and The Punjabi and his association with the revolutionaries became prominent. He left India for London in 1908 as the situation in India was very tense. In order to propagate the freedom movement further Lala crossed the borders of Paris, West Indies and South America to reach the USA where he helped to organize the Gadar movement. Sensing trouble, the British Government pressed the U.S Government to arrest him. Hence he migrated to Germany and further to Sweden and England only to go back to the USA where he passed away.

Apart from his political and patriotic contribution, Lala has contributed a lot in the field of literature and earned his Doctorate on Buddhist Sanskrit Literature. He breathed his last in Philadelphia, USA on 4th March 1939. – Ed.

[3] Although the Soviet Russia is now extinct, its education system – especially the structure and essence – should interest educationists the world over, especially India. – Ed.

4 Edict or decree.

5 Krishna and Sudama studied together at Sage Sandipani's Gurukula. – Ed.

6 To renounce the world; donning ochre robes, becoming a hermit and living on alms, devoting one's entire time to meditation and study. – Ed.

7 **Agnihotra** is a Vedic *yajña* (ritual or sacrifice) performed for the healing and purification of the atmosphere and as a primary source of *vibhuti* or sacred ash. The term *agnihotra* means 'pouring (*hotra*) into the fire (*agni*)'. It is mentioned in the *Atharvaveda* (11:7:9) and described in detail in the *Yajurveda Samhitas* and in the *Brahmanas*, such as at *Shatapatha Brahmana* (12:4:1). The Vedic form of this ritual is still performed by a small number of Vaidika Brahmins all over South Asia. – Ed.

8 *Satvic food* is one that can be digested easily and brings balance to one's mind. It helps in building immunity and improving the healing response in those who are unwell. It is closest to the natural form and includes milk, milk products, fruits, most fresh vegetables except garlic, onion, scallions, and chives. Grain cereals like most lentils, sprouts and natural sweeteners like jaggery, honey, natural oils like ghee, butter and vegetable oils are also included. Intoxicants and stimulants are non-*satvic*. The food is moderately cooked with few spices and less fat. Chillies and black pepper are not used in cooking. Common spices like turmeric, ginger, cinnamon, coriander, aniseed and cardamom are, however, used. Eating raw foods is not considered *satvic* as they harbour a lot of parasites and microbes. According to Ayurveda, raw foods are known to weaken the digestive system and reduce *ojas* (life force/vital energy), also known as *prana*.

Proper functioning of the mind and spiritual development depend on *ojas*. A person who follows the *satvic* food habits is known to possess a clear mind, is balanced, moderate in habits and focused as well as spiritually aware.

Rajasic **food** is fresh but heavy to digest. This includes non-vegetarian food like meat, fish, eggs, chicken, all whole pulses and dals, which are not sprouted. Food prepared from sour, salty, spicy ingredients increase *rajasic* qualities. Hot spices like chillies, pepper, vegetables, including onions and garlic, are all included under this category. The food is cooked fresh and is of high quality and nutrient density.

This kind of food is known to make a person long for sensual stimulation. He is usually of energetic disposition. He is interested in power, prestige, position and prosperity. A *rajasic* personality loves to enjoy life.

Tamasic **food** includes all kinds that are not fresh and are unnatural, overcooked, stale and processed. *Tamas* means darkness, implying stagnation in a person and degeneration in health. The *tamasic* personality suffers from intense mood swings, insecurities, desires, cravings and is unable to deal with others in a balanced manner. They have little regard for the welfare of others and tend to be very self-centered. Their nervous systems and heart do not function optimally; such individuals age very fast and usually suffer from degenerative conditions like cancer, heart disease, diabetes, arthritis, chronic fatigue etc. – Ed.

[9] **Lala Lajpat Rai** (1865-1928), author and politician, is chiefly remembered as a leader in India's fight for freedom from the British Raj. He was popularly known as *Punjab Kesari* (The Lion of Punjab). He was also the founder of Punjab National Bank and Lakshmi Insurance Company. Rai was born on January 28, 1865 in village Dhudi Ke, in the present day Moga district of Punjab, India.

Rai joined the Indian National Congress in 1888 and became one of its three most prominent Hindu Nationalist members, who fought for, and gave their lives during the Indian independence movement in the first half of the twentieth century. The other two were Bal Gangadhar Tilak of Maharashtra and Bipin Chandra Pal of Bengal. Collectively, they were dubbed *Lal-Bal-Pal*, and formed the Hindu faction of the Indian National Congress, as opposed to the moderate faction led first by Gopal Krishna Gokhale and, later, by Mahatma Gandhi. Rai was also a member of the Hindu Maha Sabha, a forerunner of the current day Hindu nationalist party, the Bharatiya Janata Party. – Ed.

[10] In Hinduism Sutras refer to various aphoristic doctrinal summaries produced for memorization generally between 500 and 200 B.C. and later incorporated into Hindu literature. In Buddhism it is referred to as sut ta - a scriptural narrative, especially a text traditionally regarded as a discourse of the Buddha. – Ed.

[11] In ancient times, several emperors performed the *Asvamedha Yajna* (the horse sacrifice), e.g., Sri Rama, Yudhisthira, Pushyamitra Sunga, Vikramaditya and Salivahana. It is performed to channelise the energies of the performer and to unite the people of the empire. *Rajasuya Yajna* is performed by kings in order to establish their emperorship/hegemony, to integrate factions under their rule, and to distribute wealth to many people. Yudhishthira of the Pandavas performed this *Yajna*. – Ed.

[12] It is believed that Maharishi Patanjali was born circa 150 BCE. Believers consider him to be the avatar of Adi Shesha - the Infinite Cosmic Serpent upon

whom Lord Vishnu rests. Patanjali is considered to be the compiler of the *Yoga Sutras*, along with being the author of a commentary on Panini's *Ashtadhyayi*, known as *Mahabhasya*. He is also believed to be the writer of a work on the ancient Indian medicine system, *Ayurveda*. – Ed.

[13] According to Maharishi Patanjali, when senses leave their objects of enjoyment and get engaged in realizing the true self (svarup), it is called Pratyahara. – Ed.

[14] Sage **Yajnavalkya** of Mithila (circa 1800 BCE), the son of sage Devarata, advanced a 95-year cycle to synchronize the motions of the sun and the moon. He is also credited with the authorship of the *Shatapatha Brahmana*, in which the references to the motions of the sun and the moon are found. He is also a major figure in the *Upanishads*. His deep philosophical teachings in the *Brhadaranyaka Upanishad*, and the apophatic teaching of *neti neti* etc. is found to be similar to the Buddhist *Anatta* doctrine.

The name of Sage Yajnavalkya of Mithila stands distinguished both in the *Shrutis* and in the *Smritis*. Yajnavalkya is especially known for his unsurpassed spiritual wisdom and power. The seer of a *Shukla Yajurveda* (A version of *Yajurveda*, attributed to Yajnavalkya) from Lord Surya or Sun God, the revealer of knowledge of *Brahman* to Janaka the king of Mithila and others, Yajnavalkya hails supreme among the sages of sacred memory. – Ed.

[15] *Aparigraha* is the concept of non-possessiveness, being both a Jain concept and a part of the *Raja Yoga* or *Ashtanga Yoga* traditions. The term usually means to limit possessions to what is necessary or important, which changes with the time period, though sadhus would not have any possessions. – Ed.

[16] The following are the major Upanishads:
- Isavasyam Upanishad, or Vajasaneyi Upanishad
- Kena Upanishad, or Talavakara Upanishad
- Katha Upanishad
- Prasna Upanishad
- Mundaka Upanishad
- Mandukya Upanishad
- Taittiriya Upanishad
- Aitareya Upanishad
- Chhandogya Upanishad
- Brihadaranyaka Upanishad

These ten have sometimes been called the old and genuine Upanishads. They are the classical Upanishads or the fundamental Upanishads of the Vedanta Philosophy. Some include the Kaushitaki Upanishad and Svetasvatara Upanishad also under the classical Upanishads. Sri Sankara and other Acharyas have written commentaries on the ten Upanishads only. The Isavasya Upanishad is a beautiful Upanishad. The very first line of the first Mantra, "Isavasyamidam sarvam-This whole world is covered by the Lord," induces a thrilling inspiration in the minds of the readers. Meditation on this one idea alone will lead to the attainment of the Knowledge of the Self. – Ed.

[17] Swadhyaya literally means study of the Self. The main practice is the study of the yogic scriptures but it also includes japa (mantra repetition). Not any yoga or spiritual book qualifies as proper material for swadhyaya. For a vedantin the best scriptures are the Upanishads, the Bhagavad Gita and the Brahma Sutras.

There are also many other scriptures such as the Puranas, the Ramayana, the Mahabharata, etc. Next come the books written by great mystics or masters such as Swami Sivananda, Swami Vishnudevananda, or other saints from all traditions. Also suitable are books written about these masters' biographies. – Ed.

[18] **Purdah** or **Pardaa** (*literally meaning* 'curtain' or 'veil') is the practice of preventing women from being seen by men. This takes two forms: physical segregation of the sexes, and the requirement for women to cover their bodies and conceal their form. Purdah exists in various forms in the Islamic world and among Hindu women in parts of India. However, this practice did not exist in ancient India; it cropped up in the medieval India with the onset of Islamic rule. – Ed.

[19] The Vedic Period or the Vedic Age refers to that time when the Vedic Sanskrit texts were composed in India. The society that emerged during that time is known as the Vedic Period, or the Vedic Age/ Civilization. The Vedic Civilization flourished between the 1500 BCE and 500 BCE on the Indo-Gangetic Plains of the Indian subcontinent. This civilization laid down the foundations of Hinduism as well as the associated Indian culture. The Vedic Age was followed by the golden age of Hinduism and classical Sanskrit literature, the Maurya Empire and the Middle Kingdoms of India. . – Ed.

[20] The Epic age in India is named so because some of the greatest epics came into being during this time. The epic period is estimated to be roughly from 1000 to 600 B.C E. The ancient Indian society is described in a very vivid manner in the three epics. These three famous Indian epics that were created

during this time are the Ramayana, the Mahabharata and the Upanishads. Not only are these three a part of the religious and mythological scriptures, but are also an important part of the historical roots of India. – Ed.

21 Historians differ on the origins and exact span of Indian Renaissance. Renaissance in India, it is however agreed, did not just happen in a short time, but was a continuing historical process that often remained subtle, but occasionally manifesting itself in glorious achievements. The period when the Hindu religious system was revived can be termed as Hindu Renaissance, which was marked with the restoration of the Hindu deities and tradition, known as modern Hinduism today. The Guptas, pioneers of the Golden age, resuscitated all lost glory by setting up a tradition, which was very Indian, with developments in Sanskrit literature, art forms and religion at its zenith. Continuing with the tradition, which was however lost in between, the late 18th century marked the beginning of a new era with movements essential for a complete reformation. The reformists did never think of discriminating on the basis of *jaati* (caste or sub caste), gender, or race. Hindu nationalism also rose to a great extent during this period. Advent of Indian renaissance was hence a colossal affair, which witnessed the spontaneous, yet restricted, participation of native intellectuals. Western historians describe the period within the 14th and 16th centuries as the Renaissance. However, there exists sufficient historical proof to show that such periods were witnessed in other civilisations much earlier. Indian literature in different languages, Indian architecture and Indian astronomical discoveries also date back to the first millennium with dates belonging from 0 to 1000 CE. – Ed.

22 Some of the fundamentals of the teachings of Gautama Buddha are: The **Four Noble Truths**: that suffering is an inherent part of existence; that the origin of suffering is ignorance and the main symptoms of that ignorance are attachment and craving; that attachment and craving can be ceased; and that following the **Noble Eightfold Path** will lead to the cessation of attachment and craving and, therefore, suffering. The **Noble Eightfold Path**: right understanding, right thought, right speech, right action, right livelihood, right effort, right mindfulness, and right concentration. **Dependent origination**: that any phenomenon 'exists' only because of the 'existence' of other phenomena in a complex web of cause and effect covering time past, present and future. Because all things are thus conditioned and transient (*anicca*), they have no real independent identity (*anatta*). **Rejection of the infallibility of accepted scripture**: Teachings should not be accepted unless they are borne out by our experience and are praised by the wise. **Anicca** (Sanskrit: *anitya*): That all things are impermanent. **Anatta** (Sanskrit: *anātman*): That the perception of a

constant **self** is an illusion. **Dukkha** (Sanskrit: *duḥkha*): That all beings suffer from all situations due to unclear mind.

However, in some Mahayana schools, these points have come to be regarded as more or less subsidiary. There is some disagreement amongst various schools of Buddhism over more esoteric aspects of Buddha's teachings, and also over some of the disciplinary rules for monks. According to tradition, the Buddha emphasized ethics and correct understanding. He questioned the average person's notions of divinity and salvation. He stated that there is no intermediary between mankind and the divine; distant gods are subjected to karma themselves in decaying heavens; and the Buddha is solely a guide and teacher for the sentient beings who must tread the path of *Nirvana* (Pāli: *Nibbāna*) themselves to attain the spiritual awakening called *bodhi* and see truth and reality as it is. The Buddhist system of insight and meditation practice is not believed to have been revealed divinely, but by the understanding of the true nature of the mind, which must be discovered by personally treading a spiritual path guided by the Buddha's teachings. – Ed.

[23] Mahavira's philosophy has eight cardinal principles - three metaphysical and five ethical. The objective is to elevate the quality of life. These independent principles reveal exceptional unity of purpose, and aim at achieving spiritual excellence by ethically sound behavior and metaphysical thought.
Mahavira's metaphysics consist of three principles - **Anekantavada, Syādvāda,** and **Karma**; and his **Panchavrats,** five codes of conduct - **Ahimsa, Satya, Asteya, Brahmacharya,** and **Aparigraha**. He talks of *Tri-ratnas* - three gems, which are the means and the goal. To liberate one's self, Mahavira taught the necessity of right faith (*samyak-darshana*), right knowledge (*samyak-gyana*), and right conduct (*samyak-charitra*). – Ed.

[24] One of the most famous debates of Adi Shankara was with the ritualist Mandana Mishra. Mandana Mishra's guru was the famous Mimamsa philosopher, Kumarīla Bhaṭṭa. Shankara sought a debate with Kumarīla Bhaṭṭa and met him in Prayag where he had buried himself in a slow burning pyre to repent for sins committed against his guru: Kumarīla Bhaṭṭa had learned Buddhist philosophy from his Buddhist guru under false pretenses, in order to be able to refute it. Learning anything without the knowledge of one's guru while still under his authority constitutes a sin according to the Vedas. Kumarīla Bhaṭṭa thus asked Adi Shankara to proceed to Mahiṣmati (known today as Mahishi Bangaon, Saharsa in Bihar) to meet Mandana Mishra and debate with him instead. After debating for over fifteen days, with Mandana Mishra's wife, Ubhaya Bharati, acting as referee, Mandana Mishra accepted defeat. Bhāratī then challenged Adi Shankara to have a debate with her in

order to 'complete' the victory. Later, she conceded defeat in the debate and allowed Mandana Mishra to accept *sannyasa* with the monastic name Sureśvarācārya, as per the agreed rules of the debate. - Ed.

25 **Sangharama** is a Sanskrit word meaning "temple" or "monastery", the place, including its garden or grove, where dwells the Buddhist monastic community (*Sangha*). A famous sangharama was that of **Kukkutarama** in Pataliputra. The Kukkutura sangharama was later destroyed and its monks killed by Pusyamitra Sunga, according to the 2nd century CE *Ashokavadana*: "Then King Pusyamitra equipped a fourfold army, and intending to destroy the Buddhist religion, he went to the Kukkutarama. (...) Pusyamitra therefore destroyed the sangharama, killed the monks there, and departed." - Ed.

26 Or **Xuanzang,** Hsüan-tsang, (pronounced *Shwan-dzang*) or Hiuen-Tsiang (603-664CE) traveled extensively in India. He passed through Kashmir valley, visited Takshashila, and reached Mathura, where he saw the sacred traces of Lord Buddha at Kashi. He went to Kapilavastu, Kushinagar, Pataliputra, Vaishali, Mahabodhi, and stayed at the famed Nalanda University. He then visited Rajgir and Nepal. He also toured South India and paid a visit to Sri Lanka. At Nalanda Mahavihara he found profound learning, devotion, warm and cordial hospitality. Under the able guidance of Shilabhadra and Buddhabhadra, he could study subjects like logic, grammar, linguistics, medicine, crafts and the Vedas in great detail. He collected very valuable information and manuscripts. Unfortunately while crossing the Indus River on the way back, his boat capsized and a number of documents were lost. However, some of these he was able to recover from the libraries at Kusha and Kashghar monasteries. - Ed.

27 Perhaps, Vajrayana or Bajrayana was not acceptable to the extant Buddhist orthodoxy then and thus deemed "immoral". The Vajrayana, however, is often viewed as the third major Yana (or 'vehicle') of Buddhism, alongside the Theravada and Mahayana. According to this view, there were three 'turnings of the wheel of dharma' [*[http://www.kagyuoffice.org/buddhism.3vehicles.html The Three Vehicles of the Teachings of the Buddha - at the Karmapa website]*] . In the first turning Shakyamuni Buddha taught the dharma as the Four Noble Truths at Varanasi which led to the Hinayana schools, of which only the Theravada remain today (note that the term Hinayana, which means "lesser vehicle" is considered pejorative by most Theravadins and Buddhist scholars). In the second turning the Perfection of Wisdom sutras were taught at Vulture's Peak and led to the Mahayana schools. The teachings which constituted the third turning of the wheel of dharma were taught at Shravasti and expounded that

all beings have Buddha Nature. This third turning is described as having led to the Vajrayana. – Ed.

[28] **Chanakya, a.k.a. Kautilya** and **Vishnugupta,** (c. 350-283 BCE) was adviser and prime minister to the first Mauryan Emperor Chandragupta (c. 340-293 BCE), and architect of his rise to power. He is credited with the authorship of the ancient Indian political treatise called the *Arthaśāstra*. Chanakya has been considered as the pioneer in the field of economics, having first written on the subject a millennium and a half before Ibn Khaldun's birth (May 27, 1332 AD to March 19, 1406 AD, a Tunisian polymath). He is known as "The Indian Machiavelli" in the Western world. Chanakya was a teacher at Takshashila University and is widely believed to be responsible for the creation of the Mauryan Empire, the first of its kind in the Indian subcontinent. – Ed.

[29] According to traditional myth, when Kashyap Rishi wrote the Samhita, it was not welcomed by the Ayurveda masters of that time. Jeevak, the five-year old son of sage Richeek, summarized the huge volume of Samhita and went to Kankhal, Haridwar, in Uttarakhand, India and presented the concise version of Samhita before the Ayurvedic practitioners of the time. The Ayurvedic practitioners rejected it outright, because they thought it had been written by a five-year-old boy. The boy went to bathe in river Ganga. When he stepped out of the river, he had transformed into an old man (*Braddha*). Seeing this transformation, the Ayurveda practitioners called him "Braddha Jeevak," and recognized the collected work as "Braddha Jeevakeeya Tantra". It is presumed that the time of Braddha Jeevak is before that of Buddha and Mahavira, and is different from Jeevak Vaidya, born in the era of Buddha, Bimbsaar's Bhujishya. Jeevak Vaidya was an expert in surgery, while Braddha Jeevak is understood to be the originator of *Kaumar Bhratya* (pediatrics, midwifery, and gynecology). – Ed.

[30] Or the **Kharoṣṭhī script**, also known as the **Gāndhārī script**, is an ancient abugida (or"alpha-syllabary") used by the Gandhara culture, nestled in the northwest subcontinent to write the Gāndhārī and Sanskrit languages. It was in use from the middle of the 3rd century BCE until it died out in its homeland around the 3rd century CE. It was also in use in Kushan, Sogdiana and along the Silk Road where there is some evidence that it may have survived until the 7th century in the remote way stations of Khotan and Niya. – Ed.

[31] Or **Vikramaśīla University** was one of the two most important centers of Buddhist learning in India, along with Nālandā University during the Pala dynasty. Vikramaśīla was established by King Dharmapala (783 to 820) in response to a supposed decline in the quality of scholarship at Nālandā.

Vikramasila (village Antichak, district Bhagalpur, Bihar) was destroyed by Muslim invaders fighting the Sena dynasty along with the other major centers of Buddhism in India around 1200 CE. The remains of the ancient university have been partially excavated at village Antichak. These represent the ruins of Vikramasila Mahavihara, the celebrated university founded by Pala king Dharmapala in late 8th or early 9th Century CE. It prospered for about four centuries before it was destroyed in the beginning of 13th Century CE. It is known to us mainly through Tibetan sources, especially the writings of Taranath, the Tibetan monk historian of 16th-17th Century CE. – Ed.

[32] Not much is known about this University except that it was an important educational centre in the South. Most probably it was run by Jain monks. – Ed.

[33] **Harsha** or **Harshavardhana** or "Harsha Vardhan" (590–647) ruled Northern India for more than forty years. He was the son of Prabhakar Vardhan and younger brother of Rajyavardhan, a king of Thanesar. At the height of his power his kingdom spanned Punjab, Bengal, Orissa and the entire Indo-Gangetic plain north of the Narmada River. After the downfall of the Gupta Empire in the middle of the sixth century C.E., North India reverted back to small republics and small monarchical states. Harsha united the small republics from Punjab to Central India, and they, at an assembly, crowned Harsha king in April 606 CE when he was merely 16 years old. Though Harsha was only sixteen years old when he ascended the throne, he proved himself to be a great vanquisher as well as a competent administrator. Although a Shaivite Harsha was tolerant towards all other religions and supported them fully. Sometime later in his life, he became a patron of Buddhism also. King Harshavardhana propagated the religion by constructing numerous stupas in the name of Buddha. He believed in supporting art and literature and even made several donations to the Nalanda University. Harsha Vardhana also wrote three Sanskrit plays, namely *Nagananda*, *Ratnavali* and *Priyadarsika*. In 641 CE, he sent a mission to China, which helped in establishing the first diplomatic relations between China and India. – Ed.

[34] Here the reference seems to be to the great Chalukya King Pulkeshi-2 who became famous for defeating the Mauryas and the battle with Harshavardhana that defined the southern limits of the latter's empire. Khusrow Perviz of Iran knew of Pulkeshi-2. . – Ed.

[35] **Rajaraja Chola I** was one of the greatest kings of the Chola Empire, who ruled between 985 and 1014 CE. He laid the foundation for the growth of the Chola Empire, by conquering the kingdoms of southern India and Sri Lanka in the south, and Kalinga (Orissa) in the northeast. He fought many battles with

the Chalukyas in the north and the Pandyas in the south. By conquering Vengi, Rajaraja laid the foundations for the Later Chola Dynasty. He invaded Sri Lanka and started a century-long Chola occupation of the island. . He streamlined the administrative system with the division of his empire into various districts and by standardizing revenue collection through systematic land surveys. He built the magnificent Brihadisvara Temple in Thanjavur and through it enabled wealth distribution amongst his subjects. His successes enabled his son Rajendra Chola I to extend the empire even further. – Ed.

[36] Tribal chiefs.

[37] Vassal feudal lords.

[38] Or **Sakas** or **Sacae** were a population of ancient Iranian nomadic tribes in Central Asia who spoke an Eastern Iranian language. The ancient Greeks called them Scythians. . – Ed.

[39] Editor's note.

[40] Or, Raja Bhoj Deva, the most illustrious of the Parmara rulers of Malwa, was one of the greatest kings of ancient India. He was a soldier, a builder, a scholar, an author and a great patron of learning. The Parmaras, who gained power and prestige under Munja and Sindhuraja, rose to imperial rank during the reign of Raja Bhoj. He ascended the throne approximately in 1010 CE. This is known from the Modasa copper plate inscription. He reigned till 1055 CE – Ed.

[41] These sacred threads were worn by the upper-caste Hindus, especially the Brahmins. . – Ed.

[42] Rani Padmini, the wife of King Rawal Ratan Singh was the queen of Chittor and often personified as a mythological figure for Indian womanhood and symbol of sacrifice and valor. Rani Padmini and her story has been immortalized in Padmavat, which is an epic poem written by Malik Muhammad Jayasi in the Awadhi language in the year 1540 CE.

During the 12th and 13th centuries, the Delhi Sultanate subjugated the political setting of Northern India. The Delhi Sultans made frequent attacks against their Rajput opponents, especially the Sisodias of Mewar, on one excuse or the other. The first sack of Chittor by Ala-ud-din Khilji in 1303 CE is conventionally thought to be the result of his infatuation with Ratan Singh`s wife, Rani Padmini. Ala-ud-Din Khilji received support for his seizure attempts from two of Ratan Singh`s own courtiers, who were his brothers, namely Raghav and Chetan. – Ed.

[43] As quoted by Lajpat Rai in his *Unhappy India.* – Author.

[44] Dr. Gottlieb Wilhelm Leitner, born in Budapest, Hungary, on 14 October 1840 to a Jewish family, was one of the most significant European educators in north India in the second half of the nineteenth century. Leitner's career is important because he was responsible for changing government attitudes about teaching in the local languages and he was pivotal in the foundation of the Punjab University. As a linguist, he was reputedly acquainted with fifty languages, quite a few of which he spoke fluently. At the age of nineteen, he became lecturer in Arabic, Turkish and Modern Greek, and at twenty-three was appointed Professor in Arabic and Muslim Law at King's College London.

In 1864, he became Principal of Government College at Lahore (now Pakistan). He succeeded in raising its status to the University of the Punjab. He founded many schools, literary associations, public libraries and academic journals, while at the same time dedicating himself to the study of the cultures of the Indian subcontinent. He retired from the Indian Service in 1886. – Ed.

[45] These included Pondichéry (now Puducherry), Karikal and Yanaon (now Yañam) on the Coromandel Coast, Mahé on the Malabar Coast, and Chandannagar in Bengal. In addition there were lodges (*loges*) located at Machilipatnam, Kozhikode and Surat, but they were merely nominal remnants of French factories. – Ed.

[46] Bankimchandra Chattopadhyaya's *Anand Math* gives us an idea of how villages would become epicenters of political reactions/movements in the India of those days. – Ed.

[47] **Cornelius Tacitus** (c. 55–c. 120 CE) was a Roman historian. He became governor of Asia (112–13 CE). His major works were the *Histories* and the *Annals*, surveying Roman history in the periods 69–96 CE and 14–68 CE, respectively. – Ed.

[48] **Gnaeus Julius Agricola** (June 13, 40 CE–August 23, 93 CE) was a Roman general responsible for much of the Roman conquest of Britain. His biography, the *De vita et moribus Iulii Agricolae*, was the first published work of his son-in-law, the historian Tacitus, and is the source for most of what is known about him. – Ed.

162

[49] *Homa/havan/yajna* is a Sanskrit word which refers to any ritual (practiced in Hinduism, Buddhism and Jainism) in which offerings (*ahuti*) are made to Gods to be transported to them by their messenger, *Agni*, the Fire-God. Many of these *homas/yajnas* have been forgotten by Hindus and Brahmins. In the ancient times each Aryan household had its own fire (to be kindled by the wife of the householder) where both man and wife would conduct their daily rituals. – Ed.

[50] The name Visva Bharati was coined by Tagore, drawing it and the motto from *Yatra visvam bhavatyeka nidam* – Where the world makes its home in a single nest. An interesting interpretation of the term can be found in a note on the website of the Viswa Bharti University, Raipur, Chattisgarh, "The literal meaning of Viswa Bharathi is construed as Universal Scholar, Viswa means Universe Bharathi refers to a Scholar. Viswa Bharathi is symbolically depicted in the logo, by thickly marking Bharath in the Viswa, as Bharath being the part and parcel of Viswa. It signifies and delineates that India is not confined education wise to its boundaries, but reaches out far beyond in terms of cultural and educational compatibility encompassing within its fold the real education of man and morality which is the only immortal truth in this mortal and surreal world." – Ed.

[51] **Sir Roper Lethbridge** (23 December 1840 - 15 February 1919) was a British academic and civil servant in India and a Conservative politician. He was appointed a Professor in the Bengal Educational Department in 1868, and became a Fellow of the University of Calcutta and Secretary of Simla Educational Commission. He was Editor of the *Calcutta Quarterly Review* from 1871 to 1878. In 1877, he moved to the Indian Political Department, as Political Agent, 1st class, and was appointed Press Commissioner in 1878 when he was awarded Companion of the Indian Empire. He was knighted in 1885. Lethbridge was Hon. Member of the Anjuman-i-Punjab, a Member of the Asiatic Society and the Asiatic Society of Bengal and a Member of Council of East Indian Association and of the National Indian Association. He wrote several works about India which have been considered to be of sufficient value to republish. – Ed.

[52] **Sir William Wilson Hunter** (July 15, 1840 – February 6, 1900) was British historian, statistician, a compiler and a member of the Indian Civil Service, who later became Vice President of Royal Asiatic Society. – Ed.

[53] **Yellow Peril** (also known as **Yellow Terror**) originated in the late nineteenth century as pejorative for the immigrant Chinese laborers in various Western

countries, notably the United States. Later this invective was widely used for the Japanese during the mid 20th century, due to Japanese military expansion. The term refers to the skin color of East Asians, and the belief that the mass immigration of Asians threatened wages and standards of living of white people. – Ed.

[54] The **Black Peril** refers to the fear of colonial settlers that black men are attracted to white women and are having sexual relations with them. This goes back to class and race prejudices that had taken roots under the British colonial rule in India and Africa, especially Rhodesia. – Ed.

[55] **Annie Wood Besant** (October 1 1847 – September 20 1933) was a prominent Theosophist, women's rights activist, writer and orator who supported Irish and Indian self rule. Her long interest in education resulted in founding of Central Hindu College at Benaras in 1898. Through a network of schools and colleges she tried to instill patriotism and contemporary spirit in the youth of India. She introduced inter-dining in hostels and allowed free transactions between British Indian scholars. The syllabus was a happy blend of Western and Indian philosophy, literature, history, and religious thought.

She became involved in Indian Nationalism and in 1916 established the Indian Home Rule League of which she became President. She started a newspaper, "New India", criticized British rule and was jailed for sedition. She came to be associated with rationalistic Congress group of workers who did not appreciate Gandhi's views. Mrs. Besant and Tilak worked together till his death. – Ed.

[56] **Bertrand Arthur William Russell, 3rd Earl Russell** (18 May 1872 – 2 February 1970), was a British philosopher, logician, mathematician, historian, social reformist, and pacifist. – Ed.

[57] According to the Duke of Wellington – whose forces, along with those from Prussia, Russia and other members of the Seventh Coalition had attacked Napoleon – the battle was "the nearest-run thing you ever saw in your life." (*Creevey Papers*, ch. x, p. 236). . – Ed.

[58] **Maharishi Kapila** was a Vedic sage, who had authored basic principles of the Sankhya system of Indian philosophy as available in the classical Sankhya text, *Sankhya Karika*, in 70 Sutras/ verses. Its expansions and commentaries are spread over 6 volumes. There have indeed been numerous commentaries, written over the ages, like the *Kapila sankhya pravachana Sutra vṛtti*, by Aniruddha. . – Ed.

[59] **Acharya Kanad (600 BCE) was the founder of Atomic Theory.** The founder of "Vaisheshik Darshan" - one of six principal philosophies of India - Acharya Kanad was a genius in philosophy. He is believed to have been born in Prabhas Kshetra near Dwarika in Gujarat. He was the pioneer expounder of realism, law of causation and the atomic theory. He has classified all the objects of creation into nine elements, namely: earth, water, light, wind, ether, time, space, mind and soul. He says, "Every object of creation is made of atoms which in turn connect with each other to form molecules." His statement ushered in the Atomic Theory for the first time ever in the world, nearly 2500 years before John Dalton. Kanad has also described the dimension and motion of atoms and their chemical reactions with each other. The eminent historian, T.N. Colebrook, has said, "Compared to the scientists of Europe , Kanad and other Indian scientists were the global masters of this field." – Ed.

[60] **Ghosh, Rashbehari** (1845-1921) lawyer, social worker, philanthropist. Born in the village of Khandaghosh in Burdwan district, Rashbehari Ghosh had an outstanding educational career, achieving top positions in all his public examinations from FA to MA. Ghosh was a legendary figure in the legal profession during the early twentieth century. He made a fabulous fortune through his legal practice, but donated much of it by way of charity and endowments. In 1913, he established an endowment for scientific studies at Calcutta University with an initial capital of ten lakh rupees. He also donated thirteen lakh rupees to establish an educational institution at Jadavpur, which was later upgraded into the Jadavpur University.

Rashbehari Ghosh was a Congress activist of the moderate wing. He had deep faith in progress but was opposed to radicalism in any form. His ability and contributions earned him a series of honours, such as the Tagore Law Professorship (1875-76) at Calcutta University, an honorary DL degree from Calcutta University (1884), a seat on the Bengal Legislative Council (1891-94, 1906-09), and knighthood (1915). Rashbehari Ghosh died 28 February 1921. – Ed.

[61] Born in 1867 in Ridgway, Pennsylvania, Katherine Mayo traveled the world researching for her books. As a social historian, she wrote books on such issues as lack of a state police force in New York in *Justice for All,* and the question of India's independence in *Mother India.* Mayo died in 1940.

Mother India (1927) was written in a sensationalized, almost muckraking style. It described Mayo's belief that India was not ready for independence. She based her criticisms on child marriage, young pregnancy and what she thought was the exploitation of women. The matter was greatly sensationalized and was not well received by many groups of people. The book was burned in India (along with her effigy) and New York City, and Mahatma Gandhi denounced the book as untruthful. It wasn't just native Indians who found her books distasteful, as there were many protesters in America and England too.

Much of the criticism of *Mother India* came from the fact that Mayo was an outsider, and there were several works written in response, like *Father India* by C.S Iyer Ranga. While Mayo's research was done first hand, by interviews with officials and reviews of debates from the legislature, many authors suggested that because she was not part of the culture she could not completely understand the system. Furthermore, she was accused of painting India in a bad light, and then not providing a truly viable solution to the problem. Despite the criticism, however, the minimum age for marriage was raised to 14 for girls and 18 for boys after the release of her book. – Ed.

[62]   According   to   Prof.   Makarand   Paranjpe   (JNU) http://www.makarand.com/acad/relevanceofmahatmagandhi%27seducation alphilosphy.htm , "The most significant single document in all of Gandhi's writings on education is probably the Inaugural Address that he delivered at the Wardha Conference of 1937. The Wardha conference was held under the auspices of the Marwari Education Society (later renamed as the Nava Bharat Vidyalaya) at Wardha on 22nd and 23rd October 1937... which was attended by B. G. Kher, Premier of Bombay Presidency, Zakir Hussain, Principal of Jamia Millia, Delhi, P. Subbarayan, former Minister for Education, Madras, Viswanath Das, former Minister for Education, Orissa, Ravishankar Shukla, former Minister Education Minister, Central Provinces, Jamnalal Bajaj, J. C. Kumarappa, Kakasaheb Kalelkar, and a number of other eminent educationists and associates of Gandhi. The Agenda, formulated by Gandhi, contained four propositions, which may be summarized as follows: 1. "The present system of education does not meet the requirements of the country...." 2. "The course of primary education should be extended at least to seven years and should include the general knowledge gained up to the matriculation standard, less English and plus a substantial vocation." 3. "For the all-round development of boys and girls all training should as far as possible be given through a profit-yielding vocation." 4. "Higher education should be left to private enterprise and should be to meet national requirements whether in the various industries, technical arts, belles-letters or fine arts" (Varkay 3-4). At the conclusion of the conference, four Resolutions were adopted. These had been proposed by a committee, which worked through the night, under the Chairmanship of Zakir Hussain. The resolutions were: 1. "That...free and compulsory education be provided for seven years on a nation-wide scale." 2 "That the medium of instruction be the mother-tongue." 3. "That ... the process of education ...

should centre around some form of manual and productive work.... 4. "That...this system of education ... be gradually able to cover the remuneration of the teachers" (ibid 5-6). Afterwards a committee was formed to design a suitable syllabus and to submit its report to Gandhi. This report was submitted in December 1937. Thereafter, a second Report was published in 1938, with detailed clarifications and replies to objections raised against the first Report. This second Report contained detailed syllabi for three subjects, or crafts as Gandhi would have preferred to call them: agriculture, spinning, and weaving... all these documents — Gandhi's Inaugural Speech, the Agenda, the Resolutions, and the two Reports that followed, make up the kernel of Nai Talim or the New Education, that later became famous all over India". – Ed.

[63] In 1943 the Government of India asked Sir John Sargent, the then education advisor of Government of India, to prepare as memorandum postwar educational development in India. On the basis of Sargent plan in 1945, a separate education department was established at the center and in 1946 University Grants Commission was established. – Ed.

[64] As a part of the tenth Five Year Plan (2002–2007), the central government had outlined an expenditure of 65.6% of its total education budget of Rs. 438250 million, or (Rs. 287500 million) on elementary education; 9.9% (Rs. 43250 million) on secondary education; 2.9% (Rs. 12500 million) on adult education; 9.5% (Rs. 41765 million) on higher education; 10.7% (Rs. 47000 million) on technical education; and the remaining 1.4% (Rs. 6235 million) on miscellaneous education schemes. Still, according to the United Nations Educational, Scientific and Cultural Organization (UNESCO), India has the lowest public expenditure on higher education per student in the world. – Ed.

[65] An apparatus for projecting pictures on slides on to a screen – precursor to today's projectors. – Ed.

[66] Early Germanic tribes from Denmark and northern Germany that conquered south-eastern Britain between 400 AD and 500 AD. – Ed.

[67] Or Engels were members of the tribe that had invaded eastern and northern Britain in the 5th–6th centuries and reputedly gave their name to England. – Ed.

[68] The **Normans** were the people who gave their name to France's northern territory of Normandy. They descended from Vikings and the France's native population of mostly Frankish and Gallo-Roman stock. The name "Normans" derives from *Northmen* or *Norsemen*, after the Vikings from Scandinavia who founded Normandy. – Ed.

[69] Our earliest social stratification came about on the basis of guild system. Each guild was formed by professionals who specialized in specific trades, e.g., architects, goldsmiths, ironsmiths etc. Over a period of time, due to social as well as commercial convenience people began to marry within specific professional circles – viz., a goldsmith youth would prefer to marry a girl from goldsmiths' family as it would enhance his prospects in the profession. This trend crystallized into castes later on. However, it did provide us with excellent professional skills in various fields – so essential for nation building processes. – Ed.

[70] This figure pertains to late 1950s/early 1960s. In 2003 the total number of districts in India was 593. – Ed.

Printed in Great Britain
by Amazon.co.uk, Ltd.,
Marston Gate.